MOVING OUT MADE EASY

HOW TO GET RID OF ALL OF YOUR STUFF AND MORE!

NEW HAMPSHIRE AND SOUTHERN MAINE EDITION

NANCY BEVERIDGE

ISBN: 978-0-692-39209-6

PUBLISHED BY:
RISSINGTON HOUSE PUBLISHING
PORTSMOUTH, NH
03801

Contents

Dedication

This book is dedicated to the many, many clients I have worked with through the past 34 years as a Realtor.

It was in watching what you did really well or what you struggled with as you attempted to get your home emptied out in time for the closing that I learned the lessons or found the resources that I can now share with readers to help them have a smooth transition to their next home.

This book was illustrated by my dear friend, Doris B Rice, a prominent water color artist in the area.

Foreword by Raymond Aaron

I met Nancy Beveridge back in 2006 when she enrolled in a course of study on the book I wrote called *"Double your Income Doing What you Love."* For 9 years she has faithfully focused on what she loves, which is helping her real estate clients have a smooth transition to their new home. She has grown her real estate team, purchased a truck clients could borrow to help move items and created a website of contractors and professionals she recommends to help them. She has taught seminars on "Real Estate Investing for Beginners" and " How to improve the value of your home with landscaping." Her book, *Moving Out Made Easy*, is just one more way she found to help her clients have a smooth move.

Moving Out Made Easy pulls together all the tips she has learned and resources she has found in the New Hampshire and Southern Maine area and assembled them into a guide you can use to help you organize, sell, donate or dispose of extra items. She also included an extra section on assisting aging parents based on her personal experiences with her own Mom and Dad to help all of those who are helping their parents downsize as the family homestead becomes too much to take care of. I know you will find this book very helpful and full of great suggestions. We all have too much stuff and this book has some very creative ways to recycle or consolidate our possessions that everyone can use.

Raymond Aaron, NY Times Top 10 Best Selling Author of *Chicken Soup for the Parent's Soul, Branding Small Business for Dummies* and *Double Your Income Doing What you Love.*

1

Foreword by the author

I have spent most of my professional life working with countless families who are in the process of moving. Organizing our stuff, letting go of some possessions, packing and moving forward to a new home will always be a challenging task. Organizing your "stuff", even if you are not involved in a move, can be overwhelming.

After years of helping clients organize all the necessary steps of their moves, I realized it would be helpful to put together a written guide to assist homeowners with systems, resources, checklists and other simple suggestions to guide them through the process. The book is written for the first time buyer, the move up buyer, all the way to those of you who are downsizing with a lifetime of accumulated possessions. It will give you resources for sorting, selling, donating or disposing of items you no longer use or need.

Having helped my parents sell the family home and transition to independent living in their 80's, I realized there is also another level of communication and planning required in assisting aging parents through this emotional move, so I included some extra chapters on helping others through the process of moving out. We are such a blessed people that we have an abundance of stuff in our lives and in our homes. Do not let the task overwhelm you. Just follow the suggestions I've shared and realize that moving is definitely a time in your life when you will need all the help you can get. Accept help when offered or hire help when you think you may need it. My hope is that this guide will ease your travels through the adventure of moving as you start the next exciting phase of your life.

Remember, it is always easier to travel light. Best wishes for a smooth and joyful move!

Praise for *Moving Out Made Easy* and the Realtor who wrote it:

"Nancy has a wealth of experience selling homes – and it shows!! This is a wonderfully written guide for anyone planning to move themselves or other loved ones. Also neat ideas if you're just reorganizing your own home."

Ed Facey —Hampton, NH

"When my mother decided to sell her home where she lived for over 50 years we knew we needed the right person to guide us. From the minute Nancy Beveridge showed up we knew she was perfect to handle the sale. Nancy was prepared, very professional and very sensitive to the emotions and needs of my mother. Nancy priced the house perfectly and it sold in less than a week! From there she gave us access to her network of vendors that assisted with plumbing, septic and repair needs. And finally, her office coordinated a pain-free closing. I cannot recommend Nancy and her team more highly!

Rich McIlveen —North Hampton, NH

"Everyone that Nancy has referred us to -- home inspectors, title/escrow company, movers, landscapers, etc. -- has been stellar. It became very clear to us that Nancy, as an excellent person herself, attracts similar, excellent people. They are like a constellation around her. We have heard many people say that buying or selling a home is a traumatic, negative experience. This could not be farther from our experience, and we have Nancy and her Seacoast Sold team to thank for this."

Jeffrey Friedman — North Hampton, NH

We love Nancy Beveridge! The professionalism, knowledge and worldliness of Nancy is unsurpassed. She is the best!

Jordan and Beth Ambargis, Stratham, NH

We knew the team's reputation for competency, tenacity, follow-up and bringing everything to a successful conclusion. Their level of expertise and depth of caring about every detail and every person makes them different from other Realtors. Communication at every level was timely and clear. There are not enough superlatives in the world to describe working with Nancy Beveridge; she is phenomenal and the Seacoast Sold Team is the best! Nancy went far "above and beyond" the call in every way and every circumstance.

Rose Ann and Larry Favinger, York ME

What has made Nancy Beveridge different from any other realtor is her genuine concern. She is not pushy but is extremely informative. She presents information and then sits back....waiting for the client to make the next move. I tell my friends if you are looking for someone who knows her profession without forcing you or pressuring you...call Nancy Beveridge. She goes beyond the call of duty. She's smart, creative, knowledgeable and easy to hang out with. Great person, good sense of humor and very much a realistic.

Beth Ceplenski Murphy, Stratham, NH

Chapter 1
ORGANIZING — Spend time now or spend more time and money later

The most important skill in having a smooth, efficient, cost-effective move from one home to another home is to take time to prioritize organization of 3 things....your time, your stuff and your paperwork.

Most of us do not live in an orderly, minimalistic dwelling with everything in its place. We lead very busy lives and our possessions, debris and papers begin to hold us hostage inside our homes. We feel we can never sell our homes because we can never find the time to sort through everything that needs to be done to move on. This book is designed to give you systems, resources, checklists and other suggestions to help you get through this process. It is not easy to maintain this level of orderliness. In my home it is primarily paper in the form of mail, newspapers, magazines and business files that take over every counter and desktop surface and overwhelm me. I schedule a party every few months just to challenge myself to once again sort through the piles of paper and get the clutter slimmed down. It is such a great feeling when you get rid of the extra items and you can once again see the coffee table and the kitchen counters!

The first step in moving out

Weeks before you ever decide to start the process of putting your home on the market you need to designate a few hours each day for tackling the clutter in your home one room at a time. This is the most important job of your entire move. Others can help but you usually need to at least be present.

The most efficient way to accomplish the big clean is what I call the 4 box method.

1. **Select one room to start with.** I would start with easy rooms like the guest bedroom or the dining room which often have fewer piles of debris or discarded items to be sorted than a basement, office or kitchen.

2. **Assume that Better Homes and Gardens is about to take a photo of that room** for their magazine and now look at the room with those eyes.

    - Horizontal surfaces of mantels, tables, counters etc. should have minimal knickknacks, etc.
    - Bookcases should have only vertical books and plenty of empty spaces
    - There should be no piles of magazines, boxes or other debris piled on the floor. These items should be disposed of or hidden under beds or in closets.
    - Light should pour in the windows
    - Closets and cupboards should be neatly organized and not stuffed to the gills so that you need to quickly close and lock the door before the avalanche of piled shoes and papers descends upon your head
    - Anywhere that clutter like mail, shoes, medicines or vanity supplies naturally accumulate, they should be contained within a basket, bowl or rack

3. **In center of room place 2 boxes, a large trash barrel or trash bag and a laundry basket.**

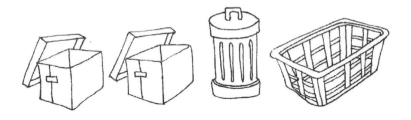

Store it   Sell or donate it   Toss it   Return it

Any item that does not NEED to be in that room has only 4 choices... you will be storing it away in a neatly labeled moving box, you will be **selling or donating** the no longer needed item, you will be tossing it in the **trash** as it has little value to others or you will put it in the laundry basket to **return it** to the correct room when this room is completely decluttered! If you leave the room you are organizing to return things that should be in another room during the organizing process, you usually get sidetracked by the items needing attention in that new room or by email etc. and will not feel that you are making progress as quickly. Having one room completely organized feels like you are making progress much more than having 3 rooms partially organized.

This process will need to be done twice. The first time you will sort items to get the current home looking its best for showings. This is when you start the process of selecting which items will be kept and stored, which items you will try to sell, which items you will choose to donate to a charitable organization or give to family and friends and which items you will dispose of permanently.

For most people this is the general order of cleaning from easiest to most difficult.

1. Dining room
2. Guest bedrooms
3. Formal living room
4. Children bedrooms
5. Master bedroom
6. Family room
7. Kitchen
8. Office*
9. Garage/storage shed*
10. Attic*
11. Basement*

These four rooms hold the largest number of unused, outdated and broken items and you should be prepared to spend more time and dispose of more items here than in other rooms of the house.

Second step in moving out

The second time you will sort your possessions is when you have selected your new home and have you current home under contract or lease. If you are going to a larger home this process is far easier as you will have more space and have the luxury of keeping more items. I would still advise you to go through the process of selling, donating or getting rid of items you no longer use or have outgrown at this time. You don't want to be sorting through a lifetime of accumulations in your senior years. If, however, you are going to a smaller space, it is now critical that you determine which items are most important to have in the new space. Make sure all furnishings you plan to bring along actually fit in the new rooms. It is a great idea to make a scaled floor plan grid of each new room to be sure the couch or dining room table fit. Very often the furnishings that were purchased for the 20 foot family room are way too large for a smaller condo or apartment living room. It is far more cost-effective to sell the old couch and purchase one that fits in the new space than to pay to pack it, move it and then find out that it is too large for the location and to then try to sell it or give it away. Often when downsizing in space, it is also very nice to have a few new furnishings so that you have something to look forward to in your smaller home.

Who can help?

1. **Grown Children:** Grown children who no longer live at home must be told that they MUST REMOVE all their childhood possessions you have been storing for them or let them know they will be given or thrown away by a specific deadline. It is not your responsibility to save their High School trophies, childhood books etc for them. They either want these items and come and get them, pay to have their possessions shipped to them, or they just don't want them.

2. **Younger Children**: Younger children are most motivated by money. Letting the children get the proceeds from a yard sale makes them far more ready to sell old toys or let go of other items they have outgrown. They need to be rewarded with a special treat to the movies etc. when their rooms have been decluttered successfully.

3. **Friends:** You probably have some friends that love to clean and organize. It actually gets their juices going to think about tossing out your excess stuff. They are excellent companions for you in this process. They will encourage you to toss the items you are on the fence about keeping. You may have skills they lack like baking or babysitting that you could reciprocate with to thank them for helping you.

*** To watch the free bonus video of how to accomplish the big clean go to : www.MovingOutMadeEasy.com

STAGING

Once each room has been decluttered using the 4 box method of sorting your possessions, if you are going to put your house on the market you may want to consider staging. Staging is similar to the process of decluttering in that you are further attempting to make each room we are about to photograph look like a Better Homes and Gardens magazine or Pottery Barn catalogue photo. You should have already gotten rid of all the excess debris, extra furnishings and unnecessary belongings. But now you make sure that little details like magnets are all removed from the refrigerator. You look at your rooms through the eye of the camera as this is how the rooms will be seen online. Look for containers under the bed which should be hidden by a dustruffle and consider ways to update or replace dated accessories and colors and furnishings. Your dining table should have a lovely centerpiece and the rooms should all be used as originally intended, meaning the dining room should look like a dining room, not a toy room.
Often furniture will need to be rearranged so that the room looks spacious and walkways are more open, even if your current arrangement is better for watching TV.

You may be able to accomplish this yourself. More likely than you might think, you may be out of touch with current trends and will probably need a professional to assist you in bringing in new accessories to update your rooms. Updating your decor and decluttering your space will make your home appeal to more people who will be willing to pay more money for your home because they can envision just moving right in without doing a lot of work.

To watch the free bonus video on staging, go to:
www.MovingOutMadeEasy.com

To assist you with decluttering and organizing spaces , locally you can contact:

Lisa Brylczyk
Organizing Czyk
Phone: 800-930-6459
Email: Lisabrylczyk@comcast.net
Website: http://www.organizingczyk.com
Gretchen Ryan
Redeemed Spaces
Phone: 603-833-7166
Email: gretchen@redeemedspaces.com
Website: www.redeemedspaces.com.

Kate Grondin, Senior Move Manager,
Home Transition Resource, Inc,
617-504-3926
Email: kgrondin@hometr.net
Website:http://www.hometr net

James and Beth Scanlon
Scanlon Senior Move Consultants
Phone: 978-479-0446
Email : Scanlonseniormove@comcast.net
Website: ScanlonSeniorMove.com

To assist you with staging your home , locally you can contact:

Pam Tiberia
Phone: 603-957-1068
Email: Pam@SpruceInteriorsNH.com
Website: www.SpruceInteriorsNH.com

Chapter 2
Selling Options: Turn your cache of excess treasures into CASH

Garage sale

A garage sale is an event in which you personally choose to trade your time and energy in order to turn your unwanted items that other people might use into cash. Furthermore, this event does not have to occur in a garage. It could be held in your driveway or in your yard. The primary goal of any yard sale is to sell or get rid of everything you do not want, so that you don't have to throw it away and fill up a landfill. Some people also set a monetary goal they hope to reach. A conservative monetary goal will help you to dramatically reduce prices once you've reached that goal and finish the garage sale sooner.

The biggest mistake most people make in a garage sale is taking it too seriously and charging too much. Don't forget that everything that's in this sale you have already decided is of no value to you anymore. There are also usually no garage sales specialists to hire so you will need to handle this yourself or give it to your children as a business learning adventure. Expect to sell items for 10 to 20 cents on the dollar.

Some of the things you need to think about in planning a yard sale are:

1. Signs, advertising, flyers

2. Tables and other display techniques

3. Items to be sold

4. Pricing, pricing labels, premade price reduced signs

5. One person to be in charge (usually the cashier who will make final negotiating decisions) and at least 3 other volunteers or paid help to assist

6. Cashier, cashbox, method of payment, adequate change

7. Parking, security and crowd control

8. Local community permits

9. Bags, boxes & newspapers to help buyers pack and carry their purchases.

10. Chairs and refreshments for workers as it is usually a long day in the sun.

Tips for top dollar:

1. People will judge your yard sale by the quality of the least desirable item for sale, so toss any item that is broken, incomplete or is in a used and abused condition.

2. Wash and neatly fold or hang all clothing. Tie pretty ribbons around groups of sheets or towels for sale. You are far more likely to sell these items if they are displayed attractively.

3. Put all parts of an item in a box or a bag.

4. Every item should have the sales price tag on it and the size of all clothing or linens should also be on that tag.

5. Price items in whole dollars, or for small items in increments of $.25 to make calculating and giving change easier.

6. Consider having boxes or tables where all items are one dollar or books are $.25.

7. Hold garage sale on Saturday mornings beginning at 7 AM as that is the time people will start to arrive.

8. Avoid major holidays, major sporting events and rainy days. In case of rain, postpone until the next Saturday instead of Sunday.

9. Ads and flyers should include the date, the time, the address and key words like "bargains galore", specific categories for sale such as baby furniture, or "everything priced to sell" and the rain date.

10. 75% of your sales will take place the first 3 or 4 hours of the sale. Make up signs in advance that say "everything reduced by 20%" and another saying "everything reduced 40%" and put them out starting at that time. The last hour have a sign made- "No reasonable offer refused" or "if you can use it, please take it."

11. Expect people to want to bargain or haggle over prices. Have pre-planned responses to their requests such as "It's early in the sale. We will be discounting this afternoon if you'd like to come back and purchase that item at that time if it is still available."

12. Have someone designated to remove all posted signs after the yard sale.

Craigslist Sales

Craigslist is intended and designed as a sales service for products to sell to people who live in your local area. Individuals may post without cost items they wish to sell or that you are willing to give away for free. A user may post content only to the single specific geographic area offered on craigslist (see http://www.craigslist.org/about/sites) and in one category. The same or substantially similar content may not be posted in more than one craigslist category.

Below are the simple steps to using Craigslist

As this is an online process you may watch a tutorial at: http://yourhomeliquidator.com/how-to-sell-your-stuff-on-craigslist

1. **Log into Craigslist.org**

2. **Choose the state where you live.** On the right side of the page, there is a list of big cities that may reflect your region. If you don't see your city there, at the bottom of the list are links to finetune your location. Click on the link that says US States.

3. **Click on the "post to classifieds" button.** It's on the left side, under the Craigslist logotype. That will bring you to a page that says: "What type of posting is this?" Select from the list of posting types: ie: for sale.

4. **Select the category** ie: appliances by owner, baby and kid stuff by owner. You may be asked to narrow down your location.

5. **Enter the posting information.** Choose your title and copy and other information potential buyers will see when they are searching for what you're selling. You must enter:

   - **Posting Title:** This is what people will see as the heading in their search results.
   - **Price:** State how much you want for the item
   - **Specific location:** Enter your town, part of town, or other general information. **Do not enter your address!**
   - **Reply to:** Put your email address here. You can choose to either display it as is, or to make it anonymous so that your name is not attached to it. This is good to do to minimize other solicitations.
   - **Posting Description:** Write a catchy description of your item. If you don't know what or how to write sales copy, take a look at a catalog or newspaper ad you might have, and see how they do it.
     Be truthful here. If there are flaws that damage the value of the item, or there's a piece missing state that. It may not help you sell, but it keeps buyers from being frustrated when they come to see the item and find these details out.
   - **Check "ok for others to contact you..."** I do not recommend this. I have found that even checking "no" that you still will get many unsolicited people trying to sell you their services.

- **Check your form.** The fields in green *must* be filled in.

6. **Upload pictures of what you're selling.** This is listed as optional, but if you want to sell something fill as many picture slots as you can with high-resolution pictures that are as good as you can possibly make them. People will seldom come to look at items with no photos. When you're done loading in images, click the **Done with images** button. Craigslist only allows 8 photos. If you are selling something fairly detailed (like a collection or car), you should consider linking to an image host where you can post more high quality images. Buyers want to see photos before they drive to your home and it helps your ad stand out. Some free hosts to consider are photobucket, listhd, and classpic. Craigslist will allow linking (text link) to other pages (with images).

7. **Check your listing for accuracy.** If your listing needs changes, click on the **Edit Text** or **Edit Images** buttons, and make any changes necessary. Craigslist will send you an email which you must respond to in order for your listing to be posted.

8. **Activate your listing** by clicking on the Continue button. When you're satisfied your ad is ready for publication, click the **Continue** button at the bottom of the page. If you have an account on Craigslist, your ad will be posted within 15 minutes. If you do not have an account, you will be sent a notification email that you must respond to for your posting to become active. Your ad will expire 45 days after you post it, but you may renew it at any time.

9. **Keep it near the top of the list** by regularly reposting the ad. It may be reposted every 48 hours.

Tips:

- Do not put your home address or home phone in the ad for safety reasons.
- Repost on a regular basis to keep listing in the first read items.
- Expect that many people who say they are coming may not show up. This is a free site.

Facebook Yard Sales

When looking to move, and therefore most likely, eliminating "clutter", Facebook can be a great tool. Many towns have local "tagline" or "yard sale" sites that you can simply post anything you want to sell or give away. You can either have the person come directly to your home, or plan to meet at a convenient place. We have had clients who have utilized these sites with great success. Do a search in Facebook for the town you are looking for to see if they offer one of these sites. Some we are familiar with are:

- Portsmouth NH online Yard Sale
- Stratham On Line Tag Sale
- Seacoast Adult Stuff Yard Sale (for those who don't have any children's items to sell)

Consignment shops

If you have a small number of furnishings or high quality clothing that you would like to sell, but which aren't enough to warrant an auction or an estate sale, a consignment shop maybe one of the easier options to choose. If you're looking for some anonymity you will want to select a consignment shop that is at least 100 miles away from your home. If that is not important to you, most communities have some sort of a consignment shop that sells used furnishing and knickknacks and clothing.

Just like an auction or an estate sale, signing a contract with a consignment shop is an important part of the decision-making process. Usually the shops will charge between 35 to 40% of the selling price if they are allowed to set the asking price. If you insist on setting the asking price, they will usually increase the percentage of 5 to 10% as a penalty. The typical term of a contract consignment shop is 3 to 6 months.

Most consignment shops have a policy of reducing the asking price on a weekly or bimonthly basis until the item is sold. By the 3rd month they may be asking 50% percent of your original asking price. You should also have an agreement with the owner of the consignment shop as to whether they will be cutting you checks once a month or twice a month, but do not expect to be paid every single time one item is sold. If items do not sell during the original contract period, pick up the items and look for another alternative means of disposing of these items.

Consignment Stores in the Seacoast

Cam's Antiques
1 Mill Street
Exeter, NH 03833
603-778-1828
What they take: Primarily lighting and some furniture. Split is generally 50/50.

My Girlfriend's Unique Boutique
same address and phone
What they take: clothing, jewelry, hats, vintage apparel
* *Breast cancer research supported with portion of proceeds*

Esta
www.Estaresale.com
67 Bow St.
Estaresale@comcast.net
Portsmouth, NH 03801
Phone number (603) 501-0136
What they take: Items for that season . Keeps them for 90 Days.
They like items on hangers and not in garbage bags. Caters to
the over 30 crowd.
What they offer: 60/40 Split

Olde Port Traders
275 Islington St Portsmouth, NH 03801
OldePort@comcast.net
(603) 436-2431
What they take: quality furniture for living room, dining room
& bedroom, plus decorative items.
What they charge: They split 50/50
If you email in photos to OldePort@comcast.net, they will let you
know if they think it is something they can sell for you. If so they
may come out and look at the items and will give an
approximate price of what they think it will sell for.

Restyled
446 Lafayette Rd, Hampton, NH 03842
(603) 926-6646
What they take: Clothing, handbags & jewelry – Vintage
clothing and all other clothing not older than 2 years.
What they charge: 60/40 Split – May bring in bags – they do not
keep hangers. Prefer to have items brought in by appointment.
They keep items for 90 days.

Second Time Around

www.SecondTimeAround.net

19 Congress St, Portsmouth (603) 433-0200

If you have new or gently used designer clothing and accessories that never make it out of your closet, bring them to STA and cash in! Usually you will receive 40% of the final sale price. Here are some easy tips to help you get started:

- Articles should be of a current style, seasonally appropriate and generally no older than 2 years.
- Articles should be in new or like-new condition.
- Garments should be freshly dry-cleaned or laundered.
- Second Time Around prefers that garments arrive at stores neatly folded in bags rather than on hangers.

The 3 Sisters Consignment Boutique

845 Lafayette Rd, Hampton, NH 03842 (603) 967-4833

T3SCB@comcast.net or Facebook

What they take: Clothes no older than 2 years. Will not take anything from Kmart, Walmart, Kohls, etc. as they want high quality clothing and household décor. Bring in up to 15 pieces at a time by appointment only. They need to be clean, pressed and on a hanger. They will also take household items and art work but no colonial items.

What they charge: 60/40 split

Wear House

www.wearhouseportsmouth.com

info@wearhousePortsmouth.com

74 Congress St

Portsmouth, NH 03801

Phone number (603) 373-8465

What they take: current items, generally no more than 2 years old unless vintage items. Must be in good condition, clean and folded. No more than 30 items at a time. Drop off or make appointment with owner to go thru them.

What they charge: 50/50 split – after 30 days they mark them down 25%, after 60 days they mark them down 50%. Unsold items must be picked up within 90 days or the will be donated.

Ebay Sales

To sell an item on eBay, you need to register and create a seller account. While you're setting up your seller account, they will ask you to review the accuracy of your personal information, confirm your phone number, and select an automatic payment method for paying selling fees and eBay Buyer Protection reimbursements.

1. Confirm your phone number

The first step in creating a seller account is to confirm your phone number. They will use this number if they ever need to contact you.

To confirm your phone number, click either **Call me now** or **Text me now**. They will send you a PIN. Enter the PIN in the **Confirm your contact information** area and click **Continue**.

If you have trouble confirming your phone number, click **Resend PIN** to get a new number. If you are still having trouble, click **Contact customer support**.

Take a moment to review your other contact information. Check to make sure your name, address, and ZIP code are correct before you start selling on eBay. Click **Edit** to make any changes.

In addition to confirming your personal information on eBay, we recommend you also start the process of getting verified on

PayPal. Because this process can take a few days to complete, it's best to start as soon as possible.

2. Select your automatic payment method

Decide how you'd like to pay your eBay fees and any eBay Buyer Protection reimbursements. You can select any of the following payment types as your automatic payment method:
- PayPal
- Credit or debit card
- Bank account

Learn more about paying your eBay fees.

Select your payment method and click **Continue**. Then, enter the requested information. Once you're done, read the billing agreement, and if you agree, click Agree and continue.

To ensure your card is accepted, make sure:
- Your credit card number is correct.
- Your address matches the billing address on your monthly statement.
- Your credit card or debit card account is in good standing.
- Your account doesn't have an Internet or phone order block.
- For debit cards, use only those with Visa or MasterCard logos.

If you need more help with your credit card or debit card, contact your card issuer.

To ensure your checking account is accepted:
- Make sure your routing number is correct. You'll find your routing number on the bottom of your checks. Routing numbers are 9 digits long. If you don't have a check available, ask your bank for your routing number.

- Make sure your checking account number is correct. You'll find your checking account number on the bottom of your checks. If you need more help, contact your bank.

That's it! Now you're ready to list your first item on eBay.

1. List it: Start by creating a listing that stands out.

Write a description
Be specific. There's value in the details.
Show off your item
Get up to 12 free pictures per listing.
Price competitively. Check completed and active listings for a price comparison.

Set a fair shipping price
Unless you're using USPS Flat Rate boxes, pack and weigh your item and get an accurate estimate before listing it to price shipping accurately.

2. Sell it

Go to My eBay
Manage your listings in one place. Track what you buy and sell, send and receive emails, view bids, and more—just look for "My eBay" at the top of most pages and
log in.
eBay mobile app
Selling from your mobile device is easy—just take a picture, upload, and list. The app is free.

3. Ship it

My eBay makes shipping simple
Get discounted postage

Print pre-addressed shipping labels with tracking numbers
Pay directly with PayPal

4. Get Paid

Print your shipping labels through My eBay to help get paid in
as little as 3 days.
Collect payments through PayPal.
Create a PayPal account

**Some people find it easier to have someone photograph, list,
sell and ship items and pay a commission vs handling the
process themselves.**

Commissions run from as high at 40% for items under $50 to a
low of 15% for items greater than a $1000.

*To date I have not been able to find someone locally who sells and ships
items for you. Please let me know if you know of a reputable ebay
specialist.*

Estate Sales vs Auctions

Estate Sales: The term estate sale is used broadly to describe any
property where there are a large number of items to sell. All
possessions are being sold and those possessions consist mainly
of antiques, collectibles, fine art, and a large number of brand
name resale items. The name "estate sale" implies there is a
higher grade of merchandise than you would find at a garage
sale and the primary purpose is to leave the house broom clean
with all items sold for a reasonable price once the sale has been
conducted.

An estate sale generally takes place in the home unless the agent conducting the sale feels the home is too small to adequately showcase all the possessions that are being sold. In that case they usually move the sale to a nearby facility.

For an estate sale, you hire a professional estate sale agent who is hired to liquidate all property within in the home. Generally you will find these estate agents more often on the East Coast or in other large urban areas. Most estate sales are 1 or 2 day events. They start off with all the merchandise marked with a price set by the estate agent. Estate sale prices tend to be halfway between a yard sale price and what you would expect to pay in an antique shop. Do not argue with agents on initial price as they know what buyers expect to pay at estate sales, which will probably not be what you paid for the items in an antique shop. Prepare yourselves that everyday antiques are not as popular with younger buyers as they once were and that many items will sell at "used furniture" prices unless they are true antique collectible pieces.

Buyers are admitted into the estate sale in a controlled manner so that there is less risk of theft. Halfway through the auction expect to be looking at making a reduction in prices of all items of about 10% and it will reach as high as 50% in the final hour of sale. Again remember that the purpose of the estate sale to sell everything.

All sales are final at the time the buyer signs their name on the sales tag and there are no returns. Your contract with the estate sale agent should be clear on who is responsible for disposing of items that do not sell and expect the agent to receive 30-40% of the gross sales. A minimum of five thousand dollars in gross sales is usually expected for an agent to be interested in the organizing, pricing, advertising, sale and accounting of items to be sold, but this may vary in different parts of the country.

Local resource:
Shannon Aubin
Asset and Estate Liquidators, LLC.
346 Bedford Road
New Boston, NH 03070
Phone: (603) 325-2991
Email: assetandestateliquidators@comcast.net
Website: http://www.assetandestateliquidators.com

Auctions

For an auction, you hire an auctioneer. Be careful to choose an auctioneer who specializes in the type of possessions that you have for sale. (Today many auctioneers specialize in selling foreclosed property, not the possessions within.) Some states require auctioneers to be licensed, but all should be bonded and this is something you should expect.

Auctioneers may be local part time country auctioneers who hold their sales in rented social halls or they may be full time licensed professionals who hold auctions on a weekly or bimonthly basis at a permanent location. Look for auctioneers who attract a large group of "regulars". These attendees are often people who resell material on eBay, at flea markets, antique malls etc.

One of the benefits of an auction over an estate sale is that it also allows some Internet bidding if the auction house is large enough to have a catalog or a large online display of the items. In this day of the Internet, the location of the sale is probably not as important as how many potential buyers they can attract online.

Expect to sign a contract with an auctioneer and be very careful that you never send any of your objects to auction without a signed contract. It is very important you clearly understand all the additional costs that could be incurred in an auction by carefully reading your contract.

Expect to pay the auctioneer a percentage of the sale price of the total items sold at auction... the gavel price. There may also be many additional hidden costs in the fine print of the contract and they can include paying for the advertising for the auction (a cost usually paid by the sellers), the cost of insuring the goods to be sold at the auction, the cost of transporting and storing items, cataloging and delivery, plus any special permits or security personnel needed. Be sure you are very clear on fees, what is being done with items that do not sell, etc. Although the percentage might be less with an auction than with an estate sale, the fees are usually much greater.

Again, just like an estate sale there is a lot of work involved in cleaning and sorting the materials to be sold. It is time-consuming, is a lot of hard work and there are significant costs for advertising. Do not be surprised if the auctioneer lets you know that you don't have enough to warrant an auction when they visit your property.

To decide if an estate sale or an auction is the right choice for you, check your local newspapers to see which seems to be more popular. Newspapers will run these ads in the Thursday or Friday editions because most estate sales are held on the weekend. If you see mostly auctions, consider hiring an auctioneer. If you see mostly estate sales that means they are a more popular means of selling these high-end antiques and you would hire an estate sale professional. Each area is different but usually one or the other method is more popular in any geographic area.

In order to conduct an auction or an estate sale, you usually need about 2 month's lead time, and if you're selling your home you often don't want the sale or auction to take place until after the property is under agreement because, most often, the property will look better with most of your furnishings in it instead of being vacant. If you are going to do an estate sale or auction, it is very important that you identify any pieces that will be offered for sale or gift to family or friends and also to box and prepare any personal or family items that will not be offered for sale, so that none of these items get advertised or sold accidentally. Keep in mind that if family members are taking a good percentage of the nicest items, attendance will be low and you will probably not have enough interest to warrant either an auction or estate sale. Buyers in general will stay away from the sales that are picked over by family or preferred customers.

In hiring an auctioneer, experience is another critical element. How long has the auctioneer or the auction company been in business? What is their reputation? Look at their web site, if they have one.

They should be members of the National Auctioneers Association.

If Estate Sale professionals and Auctioneers do not see that you have enough high end items that will sell quickly, what are your other options? Some auctioneers or estate sale agents will give you a very small payment and agree to take everything away. Do not reject this option too quickly as it costs quite a bit to have people haul possessions away. These other options will be covered in more detail in upcoming sections of this book.

For local assistance with an auction contact:

RONALD BOURGEAULT
Specialties: High-end antiques, 18th and 19th century
93 Pleasant Street
Portsmouth, NH 03801
Phone:
603-433-8400 (Office)
603-433-0415 (Fax)
Web Site: http://www.northeastauctions.com
Email: contact@northeastauctions.com

JOHN AND MAUREEN BOYD
Specialties: appraisals, downsizing, assistance consignment of personal property, estate auctions, and benefit auctions
PO Box 294
Eliot, ME 03903
Phone:
207-498-3131 or 498-3631 (cell phones) or 207-439-6641 (Office)
Email: johnboyd5@comcast.net
Web Site: www.maineestateappraisal.com

PAUL G. MCINNIS
Specialties: Antiques & Collectibles, Business Liquidations, Collector Cars & Vintage Equipment, Estate & Personal Property, Government & Municipal, Real Estate, Commercial, Real Estate, Land, Real Estate, Residential, Automobiles/ Transportation, Appraisal, Liquidation
One Juniper Road
North Hampton, NH 03862
Phone:
603-964-1301 (Office)
603-964-1302 (Fax)
Email: paul@paulmcinnis.com
Web Site: http://www.paulmcinnis.com

DEVIN MOISAN
Specialties: antique auctions and appraisals
67 Venture Drive
Dover, NH 03820
Phone:
603-953-0022 (Office)
603-953-0023 (Fax)
Email: dmoisan@rcn.com
Web Site: http://www.moisanauctions.com

STEVE SCOFIELD
Specialties: Coins and Stamp collections
Address:Conway, NH
Phone :603-548-6699
Email: Steve@CentennialAuctions.com
Website: CentennialAuctions.com

Chapter 3
Donation Options — Go ahead, make someone's day and maybe get a tax deduction too!

When it's time to decide whether you're going to sell or donate an item, it is important to consider the amount of time and energy it's going to take versus how much money you're going to actually make on the sale. To determine how much you will actually make in a yard sale for instance, consider that the average garage sale makes less than $600 and takes 30 hours of time. In looking at your big-ticket items, estimate what people will really pay for this used item and then reduce that amount by 25% if you can do the selling yourself. Reduce the amount by probably 40 to 60% for commissions and expenses if you're hiring someone else to sell it for you.

Once you do the calculations on the items you have that you want to get rid of, many people decide it makes more sense to donate the items than to go through the effort of trying to sell. There are many ways to determine how to give away your access items.

Free at the curb. My favorite and easiest option is putting it **out at the curb with a sign that says free** if you live on a well trafficked street where people can pull over and pick your items up. I always feel I made someone's day by letting them have something for free, even if I don't get a charitable tax write-off.

After I got divorced I ordered an 18 ft long, 8 ft wide and 4 ft high dumpster and put it in my front yard. I then put everything of value out in front of my fence and everything I thought was junk like scrap lumber, water damaged sheetrock, rusty nails etc in the dumpster. I had a traffic jam with people taking old Barbie doll houses, outgrown junior skis and loading every box of construction supplies or old albums into their cars without even looking in the boxes. My children were in college. I no longer even had a turntable so was obviously not playing my records. I also knew that if I ever needed electrical work done, no electrician I hired was going to go into my basement and see if I had the correct outlet to use. Yes, maybe these items had some value, but more probably they were no longer up to the latest codes and would not sell well, but people acted like they had struck gold and thanked me. Grandparents were thrilled to have old toys. Parents with young kids were happy to have outgrown sports equipment and I was thrilled to have a clean garage and basement. By the end of the day everything was gone and I did not have to negotiate with someone who wanted to pay 25 cents instead of 50 cents for an item and no one returned anything later. They even started dumpster diving for supplies they could use in tree forts etc. for scrap lumber I thought was just junk.

Another Great site to give things away on is The Freecycle Network™. The Freecycle Network is made up of 5,118 groups with 6,548,825 members around the world. It's a grassroots and entirely nonprofit movement of people who are giving (and getting) stuff for free in their own towns. It's all about reuse and keeping good stuff out of landfills. Each local group is moderated by local volunteers.

Membership is free, and everything posted must be FREE, legal and appropriate for all ages.

To view the items being given away or sought in your area, you must be a member of the local group.

Freecycle is a movement of people keeping stuff out of landfills while building a sense of community.

To sign up, go to www.Freecycle.org and find your community by entering it into the search box for the local group. You will be able to post offers of free items or post items wanted for free once you sign up for that group.

(If you have any spare time and want to watch a video on the importance of recycling versus always buying new and then tossing your old stuff out, look up the video "The Story of Stuff" by Annie Leonard who quickly summarizes the impact our "STUFF" is having on our world.)

Another huge category of people willing to take some of your stuff for free are **charitable organizations** like the Salvation Army, Goodwill, Habitat for Humanity's ReStore or the United Way in your local community. Many of these organizations will even pick up larger items and will usually give you a receipt for your donation which you can claim on your IRS tax return.

It is important to know what each group is looking for. Most of these charitable organizations resell the donated items to fund their charities, so they are only looking for items in good, serviceable condition that they believe people will purchase in their stores. Items that are broken, stained, worn or just totally no longer used by most people, like a VHS player or large suitcases without wheels, unfortunately will not usually be accepted.

Select the charity you are most interested in supporting and contact them to see if they pick up. Also make certain the items you wish to donate are items they are willing to accept.

Local Seacoast Area organizations that accept donations:

The Cross Roads
600 Lafayette Rd Portsmouth, NH 03801
(603) 436-2218
www.crossroadshouse.org
info@crossroadshouse.org
Please note, they can no longer accept used clothing donations. They have found other sources of clothing for the residents. When donating food items, please be conscious of expiration dates even on "non perishable" items.

- Diapers - sizes 1, 4, 5, 6
- Baby Formula - Enfamil
- Baby wipes
- Baby monitors
- Toddler Bed(with all hardware included; please call in advance)
- Gas cards in small increments

Linens (gently used or new)
- twin sheets
- twin blankets
- pillows & pillow cases
- bath towels

Personal hygiene products
- travel size shampoo
- travel size conditioner
- toothbrushes
- toothpaste
- disposable razors
- shaving cream
- deodorant
- diapers/pull-ups
- baby wipes
- hand sanitizer
- aspirin/ibuprofen/acetaminophen

Miscellaneous
- bike locks
- pad locks
- travel alarm clocks
- monetary donations

Gift Cards
(in low denominations please)
- gas station
- auto store
- Wal-Mart
- grocery store
- Rite Aid

Clothing
- new socks
- new underwear (all adult sizes)

Food and beverages
- powdered drink mixes
- bread crumbs
- juice and juice boxes
- salt & pepper
- prepared sauces (ie. BBQ or Teriyaki)
- sugar
- non dairy creamer
- regular coffee
- crackers
- cookies
- cereal
- lunch box snacks
- canned meals (Dinty Moore, etc.)
- soup
- baby formula
- fresh fruits and vegetables
- salad dressing
- shelf stable milk

Donations can be dropped off at any time at the Cross Roads House office, 600 Lafayette Road, Portsmouth.

Epilepsy Foundation
Epilepsy Donation Center-N Hampton
251 Atlantic Ave, North Hampton, NH 03862
(603) 379-2445

Open: Weekdays, 7 a.m. to 8 p.m.; Saturdays, 7 a.m. to 5 p.m., and Sundays 10 a.m. to 4 p.m.

Contact: Call 888-322-8209 to schedule donation pickup, or visit www.donatenewengland.org to view drop off locations and/or schedule

We're trying to attract the more family-oriented donors," said Christina Macia, director of marketing and business development for the foundation.

With its new location, the Epilepsy Foundation will be collecting donations from all over New Hampshire and Maine.

The donation center will be open seven days a week, from 7 a.m. to 8 p.m. on weekdays, closing at 5 p.m. on Saturdays and being open from 10 a.m. to 4 p.m. on Sundays.

Eighteen trucks will be based out of the new collection point in North Hampton, attending to donation pickups in northern New Hampshire and all of Maine.

Epilepsy officials selected the North Hampton site for three reasons.

"It was the road, the location and the visibility," Macia said. In addition to those benefits, the new location is also near **Savers**, which is where the Epilepsy Foundation sells the donations it receives, in order to raise money for researching a cure for the disorder.

Donations can be made at the donation center, or they can be dropped off at any of the foundation's donation bins, which are sponsored by businesses all over Maine and New Hampshire. While using donation bins or dropping donations off at a donation center are preferred, donors may also call 888-322-8209 to schedule a pickup at their home.

The Epilepsy Foundation takes all sorts of goods and household donations **except mattresses, large household appliances and products that are designed to carry or hold children.**

Goodwill Store
2454 Lafayette Rd Ste 2, Portsmouth, NH03801
603) 430-2040
http://www.goodwill.org/

Step 1: Gather Your Stuff
Walk around your home and collect items you and your family no longer need — that shirt that's been hanging in the back of your closet for three years, the toy trike your five-year old has outgrown, the holiday gift from grandma you never quite found a place for, etc.

Step 2: Give Them a Look Over
Donating items that are in working condition, contain all of their pieces and parts, and are free of stains and rips is the best way to ensure that your goods do the most good. While we accept most clothing and household items, there are a few things we can't accept – such as items that have been recalled, banned or do not meet current safety standards. In addition, if you're looking to donate specialty items such as computers, vehicles or mattresses, it's best to give your local Goodwill agency a call first to find out any rules or restrictions around these items.

Step 3: Go to Goodwill
Ready to drop off your items? Just use our locator at the top of the page or on our homepage and check the box for "Donation Site" to find your nearest Goodwill drop-off location. Donating a lot of items? Some Goodwills offer donation pickup services – give yours a call to find out what's available in your area. Each year, we also get together with our partners to offer unique donation drives, giving you the chance to drop off your items at

retail stores, college campuses and more. Stay tuned to this space for information about new opportunities to donate through our partners.

SPECIAL NOTE: Donation Bins
While we invite you to visit one of Goodwill's many attended donation centers, we understand that donation bins may represent a more convenient option for your donation needs. Unfortunately, many goods that wind up in donation bins end up supporting for-profit groups, rather than aiding nonprofit, charitable organizations.

Before donating items they will expect you to:

- Wash or dry-clean clothing.
- Test electrical equipment and battery-operated items.
- Include all pieces and parts to children's games and toys.
- Check with your local Goodwill Industries agency to determine standards for donating computers and vehicles.
- Goodwill Industries encourages businesses and individuals to donate their new and used computers. Since 2004, Goodwill Industries and Dell, Inc. have worked together to responsibly recycle unwanted electronics at no cost to the public. To date, the Dell Reconnect partnership has collected more than 200 million pounds of electronics.
- Simply take your unwanted electronics — any brand, any condition — to a participating Goodwill store or donation drop-off site. Goodwill will responsibly refurbish, reuse or recycle the equipment, benefiting communities and putting people to work
- In its seventh year, the Dell Reconnect partnership is expanding its reach across the United States, allowing more people to keep their e-waste out of landfills. As of December 2011, more than 2,600 Goodwill locations are participating in the Dell Reconnect partnership, which means more than

70 percent of Goodwill stores now participate in this program.

- To make the donation process a smooth one and — most importantly — protect your privacy and prevent identity theft, Goodwill recommends you remove all data from your computer hard drive before donating a computer, with the exception of the operating system.

Donating a Vehicle

- Many Goodwill agencies accept vehicle donations. Some vehicles are used as part of Wheels-to-Work programs that provide reliable transportation to help people stay on the job. Other Goodwill stores use the proceeds from vehicle sales to fund job training, employment placement services and other community-based programs for people who have disabilities, lack education or job experience, or face employment challenges.
- Taxpayers can deduct only the proceeds the charity gets from the sale of the car. Donors must receive a written acknowledgment from the charity that includes the sale price of the vehicle. If the charity uses the car for a charitable purpose, such as a Goodwill Wheels-to-Work program, donors may deduct the fair market value of the vehicle, and must obtain written acknowledgment from Goodwill that states how the car will be used. Goodwill must provide you with written acknowledgment within 30 days of the sale of the car or, if the car is to be used for a charitable purpose, within 30 days of the donation.
- Valuate your car based on the fair market value, taking into consideration your vehicle's condition. For guidance, use the "private party" or equivalent category in an accepted used car guide, such as the Kelley Blue Book, or consult with your tax adviser. Goodwill is not permitted to determine your

vehicle's fair market value; the tax receipt is proof that you made the donation.

Operation Blessing

600A Lafayette Rd., Portsmouth, NH
Website: www.theobnh.org
Donations: Tracy Hutchinson
Phone: (603) 430-8561
Email: Donate@TheOBNH.org

Operation Blessing depends on donations from people just like you! They accept donations in the form of clothing, household items, furniture, food, automobiles and financial donations.

Food: Food donations are accepted on Wednesday, Thursday and Friday from 10 AM to 4 PM at the Operation Blessing Center in Portsmouth.

Clothing: Donations of clothing in good condition are first sorted by volunteers, categorized, sized, and then hung on hangers. Then they are placed on display for our clients to select what they need. All the clothing is free of charge to our clients. Clothing donations are accepted Wednesday, Thursday and Friday from 10 AM to 4 PM.

Household Goods and Furniture: A unique aspect of this Ministry is the Household and Furniture Departments. Here we aid people who fall through the cracks of social services. O.B. has helped fire & flood victims, battered women, single pregnant mothers, vulnerable children, the disabled, the elderly, the critically ill, those transitioning out of homelessness into public housing, as well as those who have just been released from prison and are seeking a new start. All these items are free of charge to their clients. Your donation will make a difference in someone's life. Furniture items can be picked up by one of our delivery trucks on one of the days they are open: Wednesday, Thursday and Friday from 10 AM to 4 PM by appointment.

They do pick up on Wednesday, Thursday and Friday and cover areas south to Seabrook over towards Epping, up to Rochester and over to York, Kittery, Eliot and the Berwicks in Maine.

They do not take mattresses, sleeper sofas, big tube type TV's or anything that is not in good condition. Their needs are basic: furniture, tables, chairs, sofa, end tables, bed frames, bureaus, linens and bedding, small appliances such as toasters, microwave, blenders, toaster ovens, household goods such as dishes, bowls, silverware, etc. This organization helps people start over with items to furnish a small apartment and get them on their feet.

Savers Thrift Store
2064 Woodbury Avenue
Newington, NH 03801
Phone: (603) 427-0814
http://www.savers.com
Hours: Mon-Sat 9-9 | Sun 10-7

Savers offer the city of Newington a discount retail store that provides shoppers with a wide selection of great deals, a quality shopping experience, and a way to support others in the community through its partnership with Epilepsy Foundation New England (EFNE).

The store pays EFNE for donations made through the nonprofit or at the store's Community Donation Center at the store – whether the item sells or not.

This turns otherwise unused goods into sustainable revenue that supports EFNE's programs and services in the community.

Bring your quality reusable items to a Community Donation Centre located at every Savers and you'll be supporting a good cause and US donors will get a tax receipt.

Whether you drop off or it is picked up, they pay local nonprofits every time you donate. It's a win-win.

What to Donate

Clothing: Men's, Women's, Children's Clothing and Shoes
Clothing Accessories: Hats, Mitts, Scarves, Ties, Nylons, Socks, Underwear
Personal Accessories: Purses, Wallets, Fanny Packs, Bags
Linens: Bed and Bath Towels, Sheets, Blankets, Pillows, Curtains, Tablecloths
Media: Hardback and Paperback Books, Magazines, Records, Tapes, CDs, Videos, DVDs, Computer Software
Housewares: Toys, Games, Puzzles, Stuffed Animals, Jewelry, Crafts, Mugs, Candles, Pictures/Frames, Baskets, Ornaments, Hand Tools, Table Lamps, Floor Lamps, Humidifiers, Garden Tools
Kitchen Items: Pots, Pans, Utensils, China Cups, Vases, Dishes, Cutlery, Glassware, Silverware, Stemware, Small Electrical Toasters, Radio, Power Tools, Irons, Blenders, Mixers
Electronics: Stereos, CD Players, Speakers, DVD And VCR Players,
Sports Equipment: Bicycles, Golf Equipment, Exercise Equipment, Skis
Furniture: Sofas, Couches, Loveseats, Recliners, Foot Stools (no sleeper sofas), All Types Of Chairs, Tables: Dining, Kitchen, Coffee, End, Computer, Night Stand, Patio, Storage Dressers,

Hutch, Armoire, Bookcase, Cabinets, Entertainment Centers, Beds, Headboards, Footboards, Frames

Note: This list may be changed and/or modified as needed to accommodate business needs and trends. Some locations do not accept Furniture items, so please contact your local store for a complete list of acceptable donations.

Items they cannot accept

Unfortunately, there are a few items they cannot accept for a variety of reasons, including safety and chemical hazards, inability to repair or clean items, product recalls and high disposal fees. This list may be changed and/or modified as needed to accommodate business needs and trends.

Weapons and Explosives, Hazardous Waste, Construction Materials, Flammable Products, Large Appliances, Automobile Parts, Food, Mattresses and Box Springs, Sleeper Sofas, and TVs

Salvation Army Family Store

2458 Lafayette Rd, Portsmouth, NH 03801
(603) 427-8267
www.salvationarmyusa.org

Pickup – fill in form – satruck.org or call 1-800-958-7825
Drop off containers are all around the city.
Will not accept – VHS tapes or tape decks, No baby furniture, No toys unless in original package. Will take most housewares and clothing.
No broken items. They will take appliances as long as they work.

Second Generation Thrift Shop

9 Tide Mill Rd, Greenland, NH 03840&779 Lafayette Rd, Seabrook, NH
Phone: (603) 430-9482 Phone:(603) 468-3700

Donation hours Mon-Fri 10AM-4PM, Sat and Sun 11AM-3PM
Web Site: www.newgeneration.org

Will take: clothing for men, women and children and maternity wear. **Baby clothes are most in need of.** Books, puzzles and toys for children. Household items such as dishes, pots and pans, pictures, lamps, etc., fashion accessories, jewelry, linens. Furniture at the Greenland barn only in spring and summer.

Cannot take: TV, computers or electronics, No large appliances, car seats or cribs, mattresses and box springs, pet cages, particle board, pillows, duvet or thick comforters. No unwashed clothing with stains, rips or missing buttons.

No pickup service; must be dropped off

100% of Second Generation Shoppes proceeds benefit New Generation Shelter.

Southeast NH Habitat for Humanity ReStore
29 Fox Run Road, Newington NH 03801
(the former roller rink near Walmart)
Open Tuesday - Saturday 9am to 5pm.
http://www.nhrestore.org/
Phone: (603)750-3200
Email: manager@nhrestore.org

The Donation Center is open 9:00am – 4:30pm Tuesday through Saturday. No appointment is necessary. They also pick up! If you live in Strafford or Rockingham counties - call they can schedule a pick-up for you. The Truck is on the road Tuesday – Friday.

Acceptable Donations

- Appliances – Washers, dryers, refrigerators, microwaves, electric ranges. They cannot accept gas appliances. Must be "sales floor clean" in need of no cleaning, inside and out, electric only, in 100% working order, no missing or broken parts and 10 years old or less, microwaves must have rotating glass plate. You can find the date of manufacturer on this website http://www.appliance411.com/service/date-code.php or we can look it up for you. They will need the model number and the serial number and the name of the manufacturer.
- Architectural Items – columns, antiques, mantles, etc.
- Cabinets – kitchen or bath complete with doors, drawers, and hardware intact (please do not remove doors and drawers from the cabinets). Must be cleaned with no damage, rot, food remains, mold, mice droppings or mice nest remains; remove all shelf paper and drawer liners.
- Carpet and Pads – must be new
- Counter Tops – good condition, no chipped or loose laminate, straight pieces only with no corners, no sink or sink cut-out, minimum length 6-feet. If you are donating kitchen cabinets, they will gladly accept the counter tops that go with them if they are in good condition.
- Doors – good condition, no broken glass, no holes or deep gouges, no water damage or splintering, no lead paint; sliding glass doors must be wood or vinyl (no aluminum) with all doors inside the complete frame, not broken apart. They do not accept bath tub or shower doors.
- Electrical – lights and fixtures in good working condition, no broken glass; parts and supplies; ceiling fans must be in complete working order with all pieces intact.
- Flooring – hardwood and laminate new in the box, new vinyl rolls, new carpet rolls, no ceramic, stone or vinyl tiles
- Furnaces – oil fired only, 15 years or younger

- Furniture – case goods (wood, metal, glass) – tables, chairs, bureaus, bookcases, hutches (will not accept a hutch top without the bottom cabinet), etc., in good, clean condition and not in need of any repair, no broken doors, drawers, legs, no missing or broken glass, no missing handles, chipping or peeling paint, no rot or mold, no stains; leather, Naugahyde, vinyl chairs and sofas in good, clean condition with no tears or stains; select high-end new or like-new upholstered furniture – requires manager approval; no bedding, mattresses, box springs, sleeper sofas
- Hardware – door knobs, hinges, cabinet handles and knobs, locks. Nails, bolts, nuts, screws new in the box; no jars/cans of random nails, screws, etc.
- Insulation – styrofoam boards, rolled fiberglass must be clean with backing in place and no tears and must be in contractor plastic bags
- Landscaping – patio and paving stone, brick, shovels/rakes, etc.
- Lumber – at least 8-feet, if deconstructed must be completely de-nailed, free of rot and water damage, and free of any twisting and bowing.
- Plumbing – Parts and supplies, sinks, tubs/showers, toilets only if brand new in the box; no containers of random fittings
- Plywood – 4 x 8 sheets only
- Roofing – shingles (full bundles only), roofing paper, ice & water shield, drip edge full lengths.
- Sheetrock – 4 x 8 sheets only
- Tools – hand, garden, working power tools.
- Windows – insulated double pane glass, no broken glass, no fogging between panes, framed only (no sashes), no rot, mold or chipping paint on wood frames, no cut or broken sills, no broken cranks or missing handles on casement windows.
- Wood stoves – must be cleaned out

Items they do not accept:

Mattresses, box springs, sleep sofas, televisions, computers, electronics, appliances over 10 years old, dirty appliances, paint, stain, lead-based materials including painted doors over 30 years old, aluminum sliding glass doors, glass door panels with no frames, unassembled sliding glass or atrium doors, glass shower doors, used toilets, toxic materials, pesticides, weed killer, window blinds, draperies, fluorescent lights or bulbs, window parts or pieces, single-pane windows, window sashes, unframed mirrors, glass panes, ceramic/porcelain/stone flooring tiles, hardwood or laminate wood flooring in opened packages, used carpet or rugs, baby furniture, clothing, toys, broken, dirty, moldy or incomplete items, unassembled items, trash.

In addition to the building material donations and other merchandise they accept items to stock the store, and can always use things like cleaning supplies, paper towels, copy paper, etc., to help reduce expenses and ultimately increase their bottom line and build more homes in Strafford and Rockingham counties. When you donate or shop at the Southeast New Hampshire Habitat for Humanity ReStore all of your contributions stay local and help to build affordable housing in the counties they support!

United Way

United Way of the Greater Seacoast
112 Corporate Drive, Unit 3.
Portsmouth, NH 03801-2882
(603) 436-5554
www.uwgs.org
Donate Goods and Services with "GoodsMatch"

- **Give goods.** Do you or your company have gently used goods that you would be able to donate? Things like computers, desks, file cabinets, appliances, TVs, bicycles, etc.? Would you like to run a drive for items such as food, school supplies, diapers, children's books, etc?

- **Connect with nonprofits in need.** You can Search Agency Wish Lists or Submit a Donation. **Note that the public will not see your donation. Only the staff of their Volunteer Action Center nonprofit partners will view it.**

Their web site connects with donors and 200 non-profit agencies. It has a large list of items that are needed in the Seacoast communities. You may post your items on the web site and people will contact you. This is sent out weekly. You may write on your post that it's pick-up only. You may also look at their web site under "Organization Needs" and choose where you would like to donate your item(s). Browse Organization Needs

Sample organizations include Big Brothers, Big Sisters, Service Link of Rockingham County, Dover Children's Center, The Housing Partnership, local school departments, etc.

York Community Service AssociationThrift Shop
1320 US Route
Cape Neddick, ME 03902
Phone: 207-363-2510
Email: DMartin@YCSAME.org
Website: www.YCSAME.org

YCSA Thrift Store takes clothing, housewares, furniture, bedding, records, holiday decor etc.

These items are dropped off at the Thrift shop during business hours (10-5 daily) and sold, with proceeds supporting the local YCSA food pantry and YCSA family services.

Chapter 4
Keeping the Memories, but not the Memorabilia

Getting rid of items that were gifts to you or items which are closely associated with or symbolic of important times in your life is probably the hardest challenge of all the sorting tasks. There is a great amount of emotion and guilt associated with getting rid of these articles. In most situations, these items take up a lot of space and are really rarely looked at on a regular basis. Here are my top suggestions for ways that I have seen people deal most effectively with eliminating these possessions.

Gifts: When a person gives you a gift it is just that, a gift... not an obligation to keep it for life. You have the right to give it away, throw it away or sell it when it no longer has a place in your new home. If it makes you feel less guilty, let the person who gave it to you know that you will not have a place for it in your new home and see if they are interested in having it back for their collection or if they prefer you pass it on to someone who will love it as you have.

Photos: Framed Photos, trays of slides, videos and bookcases of photo albums take a lot of space and are rarely viewed. Here are my top suggestions for these important memories:

Photo boxes: These boxes are about the size of a shoe box and can be purchased in any Walmart, photo shop etc. They have dividers with labels for sectioning photos. I suggest you get no more than 3 or 4 of these and label each box for a period of your life or for each member of the family. Childhood, Age 18-30 (or college and pre-children days) Age 30-60(or kids at home years) Age 55 and beyond(or retirement years). Pull all your favorite photos from piles of photos, from frames and from scrapbooks and put them into the appropriate photo box. Once that box is full, that is all you keep, but believe me hundreds of childhood photos is still a lot of photos. You get rid of the ones that are blurry, the ones you can't remember who the people in the pictures are, the ones that are just scenery but hold no significance. You are left with a great collection where each photo really has a significant memory attached to it. Last Christmas my daughters got one large gift wrapped box each filled with their box of photos, every old report card of theirs, their baby books, and childhood paintings and cards that they can now share or compare those with their own children.

Share extra photos with friends and family. As you are sorting pictures into the boxes, look for extra photos to send to some of the family members or friends in the photos. Keep a pile of envelopes beside you along with a pile of notecards or post-its. As you find photos from the past that will make someone else smile, put it in the envelope as you see it along with a brief note on a post it. Don't wait until you have time to write a long letter, just jot down a quick note like "Remember the great times we had together when the kids were little? You've been an important part of some of my fondest memories! "

Donate your old frames to others or to artists and just keep the photos.

Slides and family videos will rarely be looked at as almost no one has a slide projector, video player or screen these days. If you still do or know someone who does, watch them one more time pulling out any highly memorable slides or movies and have photos made of them for your photo box. This is not an inexpensive option, so be very selective about what you save. You could also have them saved digitally on a CD if that is easier, but it will cost hundreds of dollars and may never be looked at. I took 18 carousels of slides and 20 small family videos and had them all saved on 8 discs. That opened up an entire closet.

Scrapbooks and other items of personal significance to your family: If you have more than just photos in scrapbooks, take photos of the pages and have then made into a DVD. If they have a lot of photos in them of someone in particular, say a child who is now grown, giving the old scrapbook to them as a gift, after you copy any memories you wish to retain, will be a very memorable gift.

Important parts of your home like the bookcase your husband built or important possessions like Uncle Art's writing desk which has been in the family for years are often hard to part with but sometimes cannot be removed from your home or will not fit in your new space. Capturing these possessions through a painting by an artist or photographer are great ways to still have the memory of the item, but not have the item.

Walk through your home and take photos of all the antique pieces you have purchased through the years, the family heirlooms, the handmade tree house the kids played in, the tire swing, the kitchen table, the gardens you planted, your child's baby crib or toys etc. Anything that pulls at your heart strings but which no longer is used on a daily basis or will not make sense in your new space should be photographed.

Memory Books or slide shows: The photos you took above or pulled from scrapbooks can be easily made into family memory books for all members of the household, if you so desire, online with Shutterfly or Snapfish. This is a great way to save the memories of their childhood with your children when you sell the family homestead. Photos with family members enjoying Christmas dinner with the Christmas China can be included. A digital slide show to hold all the photographed memories in one place is another idea that can be played at a future birthday or anniversary celebration when family and friends may be gathered.

Paint or professionally photograph your favorite memory: Another way to capture the memories especially if it is more of a particular scene, like a fire in the fireplace or the porch swing beside the flower boxes is to have an artist paint a picture of the scene you will most miss. Maybe you want to have a formal portrait taken of your family in front of your home or in the garden. This small painting or photograph can be framed and also made into notecards if you wish to share it with others.

Antique Photos of ancestors, family home etc.: These items go in the photo boxes also, but I would suggest having copies made of them as gifts for family members who might like them. Enclosing them in a locket etc is a very special gift, especially when given at significant life moments like weddings, christenings or birthdays. Be sure to mark who the people in the photos are for future generations. These antique photos can also be scanned into geneology software to make the family tree more interesting.

Physical mementos: But what about the HS letter jacket, my wedding dress, Grandma's mink coat or my matchbox collection?

Again I say.... if this stuff belongs to your children let them know they have 30 days to pick it up or to pay to have it shipped to them or it will be disposed of.

If these are your items, I suggest hiring someone to make a collage of these items in one frame or in a small coffee table or end table that opens up and has velvet inside. Take the letter off the letter jacket, include some streamers from your HS Pompoms, include a small fan of your favorite baseball cards, a matchbox car from your childhood, your baby rattle, the engine from your train set, a favorite Christmas tree ornament, a few old photographs of your HS prom and wedding ceremony.... you get the idea. Capture the memories with a small sample and let your brain remember the rest.

Old clothing such as your wedding dress or prom dress are rarely going to be worn again. They can, however, be cut apart and be made into something else which might get use. The wedding dress can be made into a christening gown for a future grandchild or great grandchild. Old favorite t-shirts, etc can be cut up and made into patchwork quilt throws or bedspreads or even a throw pillow cover.

Old china sets, silver sets, glassware, Hummel collection etc.: Often no one has the space or formal entertaining lifestyle to use the 24 place settings of the Havilland china you inherited from your great-grandmother. What do you do with the silver or the tea cup or Hummel collections? I suggest you have a large party served on these dishes and then have everyone leave with one plate or bowl or spoon or Hummel(which served as their place marker) to remember the party with. Everyone can handle one special tea cup or Hummel. You can also take a photo of the party table all set with all your friends around the table and give that to everyone and sell the collection if it has great value. Some people also take the items like antique silverware and have them made into wind chimes. Old tea cups can be made into candles and given as gifts. If you are not crafty go to a group of artisans like NH Craftsman or artists renting space in the Button Factory (Portsmouth, NH) and see if any of them can repurpose the items you have a collection of.

Who can help:

Make your own Photo Memory books: www.Snapfish, www.shutterfly.com

Artist to paint memory in Watercolor: Doris Rice, DorisRice@comcast.net www.DorisRice.com 603-964-9254

Where to buy shadow box tables: Furniture Traditions 714-538-2088http://americanlivingcollection.com/Living-Room-Furn iture

Shadow boxes and deep frames can often be found at antique shops also or on ebay.

Make Framed collage of items: Local frame shops often offer this service.

Portraits of home or family in garden etc: Bill Truslow, www.TruslowPhoto.com 603-436-4600 info@truslowphoto.com

Transfer photos, slides and videos to CDs and DVDs-Southtree.com, (800-656-6032. Look for special offers on Living social or groupon or at their website.

Chapter 5
Throw it Away — Sometimes it is just trash

After you have sorted possessions to determine the items you want to keep, the items you want to give away or donate to charitable organizations, and separated out items that you feel can be sold for cash, unfortunately there is usually still a large collection of items remaining.

Some of these items are damaged, missing pieces or just plain obsolete. Other items are outdated and hence no longer desired by people regardless of their condition. A lovely large suitcase without wheels would be an example of an item no longer desired.

Some items like avocado appliances or older computers can't even be given away.

Finally there is the incredible amount of pure debris that should have been tossed out years ago. Old magazines, college files, most of what is in your junk drawer or in unopened boxes from your last move fall into this category.

Your goal is to leave the home totally empty of possessions and in "broom clean" condition. The easiest way to get the remainder of these items out of the home is to rent a large dumpster and have it delivered to your home so that family members can easily deliver the items to the dumpster in trash bags or boxes until it is all gone. Smaller "Dumpster in a Bag" options exist if you have a small amount of junk remaining. Most people, however, underestimate the amount of dumpster space they will need, not realizing how much is in the attic, the basement, under the deck, behind the garage or in the closets.

Having family members empty the possessions into the dumpster decreases the likelihood that items of value or personal significance will be accidentally thrown away. Family members who are not available to help with this difficult task need to understand that some items may be tossed out that they would have kept, but that the disposal process has to be done in a timely manner.

Sometimes you do not have the manpower, time or strength available to actually empty the home and fill the dumpster yourselves. Fortunately there are junk disposal services which will actually bring the dumpster and empty the household debris into the dumpster and take it away for a fee. There are also organizations which will perform what is called a "whole house cleanout" where they take away items they can sell and dispose of the remainder. This arrangement may be easiest for families with very little time to sort, sell, donate and dispose of a household of possessions and debris.

Salvage: One thing to think about before throwing everything remaining in the dumpster is to recognize that not all junk is trash. Some of the items may be made of materials which can be picked up by or sold to local salvage yards. Base metals such as aluminum, brass, steel, cast iron, tin, copper and zinc are found in many household items like pipes, pots and pans, tools. Metals, however, must be sorted or you will receive payment for the least expensive metal in the pile. Copper right now is very valuable, but that means you need to remove the copper bottoms of pans from the top section to get paid for the copper in a pan. Natural fabrics like cotton or wool (not synthetics) can be found in old clothing, linens etc and may be able to be sold or recycled to a textile dealer.

Be sure to check with your local salvage yard or textile dealer to see what they are taking and what they are paying per pound before you go to the effort of separating these items from your other junk. It may not be worth the time and effort you put into it.

Dumpster Resources

Waste Management
Phone: 603-929-4500
Web Site: www.wm.com

15 yd - Portsmouth area - $750 +/-
14'Lx8'Wx4'H – equal to F150 Pickup truck 6-7 loads.
Cost includes: delivery, removal and environmental fee for up to 2 tons for two weeks.
Additional $95 a ton after that at $10.00 per day.

30 yd Portsmouth area $825 +/-
Cost includes delivery, removal, and environmental fee for up to 3 tons for 2 weeks.
Price depends on fuel pricings and location to landfill.

The following items cannot go in a dumpster:
- Anti freeze
- Car batteries
- Computer or computer parts

61

- Florescent lights
- Tires
- Paint, oil, gas or motor oil
- Propane tanks
- Asbestos
- 50 gal drums
- Air conditioners
- Freezers
- Copiers
- Smoke detectors
- Major appliances (refrigerator, stove, dishwasher, washer, dryer)
- Mattresses
- TV, computers or monitors

Thebagster.com

The WM Bagster Dumpster in a Bag is the perfect on-demand waste removal solution for your job site or do-it-yourself project. Go to Home Depot, Lowes or Ace Hardware and buy bag for approximately $29.95. Fill the bag with up to 3,300 lb. of debris or waste, and then schedule your collection with Waste Management. The collection fee is not included. Pick up will run in the $120-$165 range. Visit www.thebagster.com or call 877.789.2247 to confirm your location is within the collection service area.

- Disposable bin for trash, refuse and waste
- 3,300 lb. capacity
- 2-1/2 ft. H x 4 ft. W x 8 ft. L
- No lid
- Collection Service not available in all markets
- Collection fee varies by market and is paid to local waste provider prior to pick up

Great Rate Container Service, LLC
414 Rte 125, Brentwood - 603-236-7477
Accredited through the Better Business Bureau with an A+
rating
www.greatratecontainer.com
email: greatrate@comcast.net
Why Choose Them?
- Free Estimates, primarily provide dumpsters on site, but also labor if needed to load dumpster.
- Low Rates & No Hidden Charges, Discounted Packages Available
- Everything Is Recycled if possible
- Personal Service
- Locally Owned & Operated

1-800gotjunk.com
Web Site: www.1800gotjunk.com
Check price and pick-up times online or call 1-800-468-5865.

1-800-GOT-JUNK? is your full-service junk removal company. They offer junk removal services for your home or business including offices, retail locations, construction sites, and more. They're the junk removal company that handles the tough stuff – and ensure that your junk gets recycled, donated, or disposed of responsibly.

Got old furniture, appliances, electronics, tires, construction debris, or yard waste you need to make disappear? 1-800-GOT-JUNK? can take away almost any material they can fit in their trucks, without you ever lifting a finger. They'll remove junk from wherever it's located, and they won't leave a dent or speck of dirt behind.

When they say they're your full-service junk removal company, they really mean it.

Choosing 1-800-GOT-JUNK? as your junk removal company is simple. Here's how this junk removal service works:

Book a no-obligation appointment online or call 1-800-468-5865. They offer same-day service and their uniformed truck team will call you 15-30 minutes before your scheduled 2 hour arrival window.

When they arrive, just point to the junk you want removed and their uniformed truck teams will provide you with an upfront, all-inclusive price.

They load all the items you want removed – wherever they are located – into their truck, and finish by cleaning up the area.

It's not just junk to them! They do their best to donate and recycle as much as they can. Since 1989, they've saved over 1.5 billion pounds of junk from the landfill, and counting.

Whole House Cleanout Services
Daryl Pelletier
DPelletier213@gmail.com
603-860-2308
Specializes in coming in and doing a whole house cleanout, where he can buy or help you sell items of value and/or haul away all the items which will not probably sell.

Junk Removal
Art McConnell - 207-351-5282
No Web Site
e-mail junkieent@aol.com
P.O. Box 170, York Harbor, ME 03911
Typically charges $500 to $600 per 20 yard load on house clean outs depending on the material being taken out & the amount of labor involved.

Jim's Pick Up Service
Jim Carney - 603-642-8996
Junk Removal
Fremont, NH 03844
http://www.jimspickup.com
Call for Estimate Mon-Sat, he says he offers reasonable rates

Scrap Metal Salvage Companies

Harding Metals, Inc.
P.O. Box 418, Northwood, NH.
(603) 942-5574 (800) 370-5865
This full-service metal recycling company consistently offers fast, comprehensive and professional scrap metal recycling services to individuals and businesses throughout New Hampshire and beyond. Since 1963, Harding Metals, Inc has enjoyed a well-deserved reputation as being one of the top scrap metal dealers in New England. This 100-acre facility features top-rate scales and is in compliance with all federal and state guidelines regarding system monitoring.

All quantities of industrial scrap metal are handled by this fully-licensed New Hampshire scrap metal dealer, with comprehensive record-keeping always provided. On-site consultations and evaluations are offered by Harding Metals, Inc, as are container services and scrap metal management programs. This New Hampshire scrap metal dealer maintains a large fleet of trucks but only offers pick-up service for commercial accounts. Competitive prices are always paid by Harding Metals, Inc.

Schnitzer Madbury
290 Knox Marsh Road, Madbury, NH 03823
phone: 603-749-3314

Located off NH-16 (Spaulding Turnpike), NH-9, ME-101

Open Monday through Friday, Schnitzer Madbury - regularly accepts all types of ferrous and non-ferrous metals. They purchase scrap metal from individuals, industrial manufacturers, railroads, auto salvage yards, metal dealers and other sources. Schnitzer Madbury consistently provides fast, professional service.

I did not find a local textile dealer who purchased cotton or wool fabrics in the Seacoast Area.

Chapter 6
Packing and Storing

Supplies to buy for the move

Do it Yourself Packing materials:
- Packing tape and dispenser 6-8 rolls of clear (not duct) tape
- Packing boxes of various sizes:
- 10-20 small packing boxes
- 10 book boxes
- 10-20 medium boxes
- 5 wardrobe boxes
- 10 picture and mirror boxes
- Black Markers to label boxes
- Heavy duty Zip lock baggies - small and large for parts, cords, screws etc from electronics or appliances. Tape bag to inside of appliance if possible.
- Stretch wrap to wrap upholstered furniture
- Box cutters to make opening and breaking boxes down easier
- Newspapers or packing paper - Save at least a foot of newspapers or buy packing paper
- Contractor grade large trash - 1 box for misc linens, clothes, pillows, etc.

- Large adhesive labels for boxes - to label room and contents
- A velcro back belt to save your back from heavy lifting
- Tools for assembly and disassembly, flat and phillips head screwdrivers, hammer, pliers
- Gloves - Heavy work gloves and also latex gloves are helpful
- Furniture pads: (can be rented with truck) to wrap wooden furniture in, 2 per item wrapped
- Newspapers or packing paper - Save at least a foot of newspapers or buy packing paper
- Floor protection rolls of paper or plastic for covering main pathways of home on moving day
- Ropes or ties to secure items in a truck
- Paper Plates, Paper Towels, Plastic silverware, Plastic cups- for moving day
- Case of water bottles or Gatorade, snacks and first aid kit - to keep workers going

Rent or purchase:
- Dolly - preferably with straps to move large items and piles of boxes to curb
- Wheelbarrow or cart for getting heavy or messy items to curb or dumpster
- Furniture pads: (can be rented with truck) to wrap wooden furniture in, 2 per item wrapped
- Wheelbarrow or cart for getting heavy or messy items to curb or dumpster

Make an Open me first survival box for each major room

Bedrooms
- Alarm clocks or clock radios
- Favorite toys, bedtime books for kids
- Pajamas and change of clothes for next day
- Sheets and pillows

Kitchen
- Cell phone chargers
- Coffee, coffee pot, filters if needed
- Can opener, wine opener
- Cleaning supplies like sponges, Windex, paper towels, dish towels
- Dishware - Set of plates, glasses, silverware, coffee mugs, or plenty of paper products and plastic silverware
- First aid kit with medicines, kleenex, bandaids
- Light bulbs
- Pet food
- Snacks, drinks
- Telephone and answering machine
- Toilet paper
- Tool kit with 3 box cutters, hammer, phillips and flat head screwdrivers, wrench, pliers,
- TV remote controls

Bathroom
- Toilet paper
- Bath towels
- Tissues
- Important medicines, basic first aid kit

What Papers and other items are best to stay with you in the car

Having the following items in the car will make the move much smoother and eliminate hassles if shipment is delayed or damaged or lost. Keep the items with the most sentimental value with you for peace of mind, but be sure to secure and hide them safely in your car.

Papers
- Airline Tickets
- Car keys

- Cell phones and chargers
- Checkbooks
- Insurance records with contact phone numbers and account numbers
- Copy of HUD settlement statement from sale of first home as it will be required at the closing if you are going to be purchasing your next home.
- School records
- Pet health records
- Maps
- Medicine, needed regularly
- Address book and phone book
- Back up discs of computer files, financial records
- Small portable iPad or tablet to use before rest of computer equipment arrives and is set up
- List of all online user names and passwords for accessing online accounts, email etc.

Valuables
- Jewelry, special pieces
- Irreplaceable photos, wedding album, etc
- Sterling silver
- Coins, stamp collections in fireproof locked box
- Stock certificates, bonds, IRA info in fireproof locked box

Hazardous or prohibited items which cannot be moved
Whether you are using a professional mover or doing the move yourself, most of these items will not be allowed on the truck or if they are allowed they will limit your mover's liability if something is damaged. Consider moving them in your car, or not moving them at all.

Hazardous
- Compressed gases like propane tanks or camp stove cannisters
- Corrosive or radioactive materials
- Explosives
- Flammable liquids or solids
- Loaded guns
- Poisons

Common Household materials usually not taken by movers (get a list from your mover to be sure)
- Aerosol cans (hairspray, cleaners, etc)
- Ammonia, bleach, vinegar, dishwashing liquids, laundry detergent
- Batteries
- Champagne
- Fire extinquisher
- Matches, stick lighters
- Motor oil
- Nail Polish remover
- Opened bottles of wine, beer, alcohol
- Paint, paint thinner. (Ask new owner if they want remaining usable paint that matches current paints on home. Do not assume they want them. If they do not you will need to get rid of them as even the trash people will not take them. The easiest way to get rid of them is to buy large rolls of plastic sheeting, spread it out, spill remaining paint on sheets and toss plastic once paint has dried. If there is just a small amount of paint left you can usually add kitty litter and it will dry up and become solid.)
- Pesticides, weed killers and fertilizers (again, not easy to throw in trash. Most towns have a hazardous waste disposal day once or more a year, so check with town hall for how to get rid of these items in a safe manner.)

Moving In Day

1. If at all possible, have cleaning people clean insides of drawers, cabinets, closets, etc and also totally sweep out the basement, attic and garage floors the day before the movers deliver furniture. This will allow you to immediately put clothing and dishes etc away. Because it is very hard to keep recently shampooed carpets clean, I recommend having those done after the furniture is in the rooms.

2. Be sure you have someone whose full time job for the day is to watch young children and pets, or make plans for children and pets to be somewhere else.

3. Start by taking the head mover on a tour of the new home so they know where each room is. Label each room of the house to match the labels on the boxes so movers know which is the correct room to deliver each box.

4. Draw a simple floor plan with a desired furniture layout of all rooms and tape it to the entrance to that room. Movers will not appreciate moving furniture over and over again.

5. Movers (paid or volunteers) always will appreciate you providing snacks, pizza and bottles of water throughout the day as they work hard.

6. Designate one member of the family to be in charge of directing movers. That person meets each mover as they get off the truck and check each box or numbered item off on the inventory checklist.

7. At the end of the day you will be asked to sign or initial each page of the inventory list before he leaves. Be sure to sign

"subject to inspection" so that you have time to inspect each box and item thoroughly within the time frame given for filing any claims.

Deciding whether to pay to rent a storage unit for your extras

Renting a storage unit is a great way to store items you don't have room for at home, but are rental units really worth the monthly fee? The answer depends on a number of factors. The price to rent a storage unit varies greatly according to size and available options, but depending on what you're storing and how long you're storing it, renting a space may or may not be worth the cost. The following information will help you decide if it's worth the money to rent a storage unit on a long-term basis.

People rent storage units for a variety of reasons. Some don't have room for extra belongings when moving to a smaller home, and others store items in order to keep them until they can be retrieved at a later date. Whatever the reason you're considering renting a place for storage, it's important to consider whether it's financially wise to do so in the first place.

Consider This

For example, if you plan on storing items such as furniture of average quality, seasonal decorations, yard tools, and other miscellaneous household items, for a basic 10 foot by 20 foot storage unit you'll pay approximately $60 a month, depending on the rates in your particular area. This doesn't seem like much, but it works out to $720 a year, and if you rent a space at this rate for 3 years, you'll spend a grand total of $2,160. Most people don't think about the total cost of long-term storage, and when they really stop to consider what they've spent after renting a storage unit, they realize they could have purchased new items with the money wasted on storing the old ones.

Can Your Items Be Replaced?

When trying to decide if renting a storage unit is wise, consider the value of the items you intend to store, as well as the length of time you plan to store them. It might be wiser to sell the items or give them to charity rather than pay monthly storage rental fees. Depending on the items you plan to store, you might be better off spending the money for new items once you have room for them, rather than throwing the money away each and every month. I don't know about you, but I'd rather put $2,160 toward new furniture than store old furniture for three years. Unless you're storing high-cost items or belongings that are irreplaceable, renting a storage unit probably isn't worth the cost.

Costs of Storage Units

Please look closely at the value of the items you decide to keep and put in a storage unit.

- A 5x5 ft. unit can cost between $40 and $50 per month. A 10x15 ft. unit can cost between $75 and $140 per month. A 10X20 ft. unit can cost between $95 and $155 per month. A 20x20 ft. unit can cost around $225 per month.

Climate Controlled
- Storage units that are climate-controlled can demand a higher price tag. For example, a 10x15 ft. climate-controlled unit can cost between $115 and $150 per month. A 10x20 ft. climate-controlled unit can cost between $170 and $180 per month.

Portable
- Some storage units are portable such as POD (portable on-demand) storage units. A 8x8x12 ft. POD unit can cost the consumer around $230 per month.

Additional Costs
- Usually, consumers will have to make a one-time purchase of some type of lock for their storage unit. Heavy-duty locks can cost upwards of $20 apiece. Some storage unit facilities may require security deposits on their storage units.

Late Fees
- If rent is not paid on time, the owners of the storage unit have the right to charge late fees. According to Storage Locator, late fees are usually reasonable, but vary widely from facility to facility.

What should be included:
- Self storage centers should have security measures including gating and onsite monitoring.
- Climate control typically means keeping the temperature below 90 degrees in the summer and above 40 degrees in the winter, with humidity below 65 percent to stop mold or mildew, according to Inside Self Storage magazine. Climate

controlled units are generally used for pianos, photographs and art items.
- Portable on demand units are delivered to the home for the renter to pack. They are taken to a storage facility or delivered to the new destination for unpacking.

Additional costs:
- Padlocks are required and may be purchased at the storage facility or supplied by the renter. Heavy duty weatherproof locks run $16-$20.
- A security deposit around $30 may be required at some sites.

Discounts:
- Some companies offer seasonal and move-in discounts like "first month free" for new tenants.
- Senior discounts around 10% are available at several locations.

Shopping for self storage:
- The Self Storage Association offers an online locater for finding a self storage facility.
- Cudahy self storage offers an online space calculator to determine the size of unit needed.

Storage Facilities in the local area

Heritage Storage Center
70 Heritage Ave, Portsmouth, NH 03801 (603) 433-1211
http://www.storuself.com/
Apartment & Condominium Owners
Extra space for seasonal clothing, skis, bikes and lawn furniture.
Homeowners
Whether you are selling your current home or have just run out of space.
Storage for family heirlooms

Free up garage space and store your motorcycle, snowmobile, extra furniture and seasonal gear.
Selling your home? Make it more presentable by opening up space.

Students
Going home for the summer and need somewhere to store your valuables?
Relocating
Use Stor-U-Self for temporary storage while you're in between residences.
They offer 20 foot and 40 foot container storage. These can be used on their site or delivered to your site.
Commercial:
Contractors - store tools, equipment and building materials!
Personal:
Container storage is perfect for storing automobiles, motorcycles, snowmobiles and larger seasonal items.
Save your money! Don't rent a truck! They'll let you use theirs when you move in.
Boxes & Supplies - Boxes, Locks, Mattress Bags/Plastic Covers, & Packing Supplies.

Hauch Storage
2185 Woodbury Ave, Newington, NH 03801 (603) 431-2749
Eagle Storage - Dover
221 Knox Marsh Rd, Dover, NH 03820 603-750-7500
390 Main St, Somersworth, NH 03878 603-692-6400

Lafayette Self Storage
330 West Rd, Portsmouth, NH 03801 (603) 431-8747
website:http://www.lafayetteselfstorage.net
email: support@lafayetteselfstorage.net

A1 Self Storage
Portsmouth, NH 03801 (603) 431-2077

STORAGE PODS
local: Greater Southern New Hampshire Area Storage Center:
140 Burke St, Nashua, NH 03060
http://pods.com/
phone:888-371-9473

PODS (Portable On Demand Storage) offers portable moving and storage services in the United States, Canada and Australia. These are sometimes used just for storage and sometimes they are a blend between Do It Yourself moves and professional movers. They can deliver an empty container which you pack, and then the container can be stored at a storage center.

Whether you need local moving, local moving with storage, long distance moving or long distance moving with storage, they can help. Use their storage calculator to determine the best PODS size that fits your needs. In some instances, it may be necessary to rent more than one container to accomplish your goals.

Chapter 7
Movers — how important is your back?

Do It Yourself

If you decide you want to handle the move yourself, here are a few things to think about:

How regularly do you lift weights; are you are sure you can do it without hurting yourself and how important is your back?

How many really good friends or family members do you have with the time and the strength to help you move boxes and heavy pieces of furniture?

How many flights of stairs are involved to get items out and then into the new dwelling?

Do you have access to a weather tight truck, ramps, dollies, tie-down ropes, boxes and winches? Most often it will take one whole day just to get items out of the first house and a second whole day to get them into the new house, so the things will have to stay in the truck overnight.

How much time do you have available away from work to be involved with the process of packing, moving and unpacking your possessions? (You will find that simply sorting through and disposing of unnecessary, outgrown or broken items in your basement, garage, attic or storage bin is a full-time job.)

What does it cost to rent the above items?
Usually you are under a deadline because of a closing or the end of a lease so there is usually little room for delays.

What responsibility will you need to assume if a friend or family member is injured helping you during the move?

Who will be taking care of the pets and children during the moving process?

Does insurance cover your possessions if they are lost or damaged during a self-move?

If you decide that you still want to do a move yourself, you will most likely need to rent a truck or get a portable storage unit that you can load over time.

If you have packed yourself but need help carrying items out of your current residence and/or into your new home, consider Labor Ready Pool to find workers to assist you.

STORAGE PODS
U-Box® pods for moving & storage
The U-Box is a revolution in how you can move. A U-Box pod fits about a room and a half of household items. If you got it into your house, you can get it into a U-Box.
Save time, save money, and have peace of mind while moving
http://pods.com/

PODS (Portable On Demand Storage) offers portable moving and storage services in the United States, Canada and Australia. Storing for 3 months or longer? Save big with their special bundle pricing. Save 10% when you reserve a container online.

Portable moving containers are delivered to your residence or business for you to fill at your own pace. Store it on site or call them when ready and they will come pick up your container and drive it to any destination you choose. Or they can store your possessions in a safe, secure and affordable storage facility for as long as you need. Find PODS storage units in your local area at www.pods.com.

Whether you need local moving, local moving with storage, long distance moving or long distance moving with storage, they can help. Use their storage calculator to determine the best PODS sizes that fits your needs. In some instances, it may be necessary to rent more than one container to accomplish your goals. Either way, they are here for your personal or commercial needs.

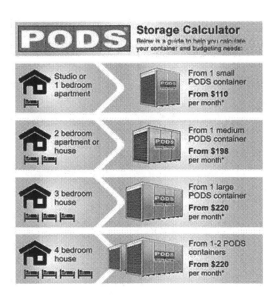

PODS containers are available in 3 sizes that can accommodate a small apartment all the way up to a large residential home. If you require commercial services, you may need more than one moving container to complete the job. It's important to choose the right portable storage unit for your particular residential or commercial situation. Either way, they have the solution for you.

With their innovative products and services, it eliminates the need for traditional storage units, moving truck rentals, travel time between facilities and time loading and unloading your possessions. For a limited time, save 10% when you reserve PODS storage units online. No long term contracts, month to month agreements and pay as you go. Get a quote or reserve a unit online.

U-Haul Moving & Storage of Portsmouth
400 US Highway 1 Bypass, Portsmouth, NH 03801 (603) 431-2165
http://www.uhaul.com/locations/truck-rentals-near-portsmouth-nh-03801/790059

Moving to or from Portsmouth, NH, 03801? Get FREE truck rental rate quotes at U-Haul Moving & Storage of Portsmouth. U-Haul rental trucks are specifically engineered from the ground up to assist moving families, not freight. They report that their moving trucks have more safety features than other moving trucks in the industry including gentle ride suspension and high visibility mirrors to assist the driver. Whether you are moving a smaller apartment or a large four-bedroom house, U-Haul truck rentals in Portsmouth, NH will provide you with the moving truck rental you need to get from point A to point B. Find the perfect size moving truck to assist with your move, U-Haul is home of the $19.95 rental truck!

U-Haul storage facility features
- Clean, dry and secure facilities
- Open 7 days a week, evenings and holidays
- 24-hour access at most locations
- Climate control available
- No deposit, make payments online
- SafeStor self-storage insurance available
- *One month free self-storage with one-way equipment rentals

In an effort to help you better prepare for your upcoming move, they have put together some tips that we know will help. These tips can help save you time as well as money.

How to select a Moving Company

This is a large investment and the moving company you select will be transporting your entire accumulation of life possessions, so it would be prudent to interview and get 3 quotes. Some questions to ask movers are as follows.

1. Are they registered with the government, what is their DOT number?

2. How do they determine their estimates and how do they determine the actual cost? Is the estimate binding, not to exceed? If not, how far apart could those figures be?

3. What supplies are included in the estimate? Furniture pads, cartons, bubble wrap, crates?

4. Are there any extra fees for anything...moving certain items like a piano, carrying items up stairs or in an elevator, fuel charges, tolls etc.?

5. Do movers take apart and reassemble beds and other large pieces of furniture at each end as part of quote?

6. What form of payment will be required at the delivery of the goods?

7. Will your possessions stay in one truck from pickup to delivery?

8. What insurance coverage is included and can it be increased? Do they have workman's comp for employees?

9. If you pack items yourself, what containers are acceptable and does the insurance policy cover items you pack?

10. How do they protect the property you are leaving and the property you are moving into from damage?

11. When will your belongings be delivered to your new home?

12. What is your procedure for claims?

13. If storage is included, is it climate controlled?

Getting ready for the moving company

Tips acquired from William C Huff Moving and Storage

Decide What Goes. Many times people move things to their new homes, which they really will never use again. A great rule of thumb is "When in doubt, throw it out." In other words, if you have not used or even seen something for a few years, maybe you can do without it.

Irreplaceable / Valuable Items. It is often best if you move your precious goods, such as jewelry and family heirlooms in your own vehicle when at all possible. If movers take these items, a detailed inventory and a certified valuation should be done prior to the move date.

Dressers and Drawers. You may leave clothing and linens in dresser drawers; however, you should remove all breakable items and liquids. Paper goods, magazines and files should be removed and packed prior to moving.

Lamps and Pictures. These items need to be moved in boxes. You must notify moving company in advance if you want them to box these items, or move them yourself.

Particle Board/Assembled Furniture. If you have furniture (computer desk, entertainment center, storage chest, etc.) that came in a flat box and required hours of assembling, these pieces were not meant to be picked-up, carried, put on a truck and delivered in their assembled form. It is best for these items to be completely disassembled prior to move.

Heavy Glass/Valuable Artwork. These items need to be crated. An appointment is needed to have exact measurements taken.

Storage Areas/Attics/Sheds/Basements. These areas tend to be extremely time consuming and expensive for movers to move. You will save a lot of time and money if these areas are presorted or moved ahead of move day.

Electronics. Disconnect and pack stereo equipment, DVD players, TVs, computers and other sensitive electronics before move day, hopefully in their original boxes. Plasma and LCD TV's will need to go into their original box or a crate will need to be built for their protection.

Boxes. Please use smaller "book" boxes for books and papers because of weight. Mark "FRAGILE" on delicate items and always seal the top and bottom with proper packing tape. Mark your boxes with its contents and intended location in your new home.

Washers/Dryers/Fridges/Chandeliers. Movers usually do not disconnect any gas, plumbing or electrical items. This needs to be done in advance by a licensed contractor. Plan to disconnect plumbing lines from your washing machine prior to your move in the event of leaks.

Personal and Last Minute Items. Pack any necessities you may require while moving or getting settled after your move such as: cell phone, change of clothes, toiletries, financial information, or any paperwork needed for a closing, etc. Put these items in a box or bag and keep it with you so you have them at your new home.

Prohibited Items. DOT and insurance regulations prohibit transporting such items as: firearms, flammable liquids or caustic / corrosive chemicals. Also, we would recommend that you move any liquids such as soaps, cleaning supplies and any paints yourself.

Placing Furnishings. You will save a lot of time and money if you are at the destination point directing movers where items are to be placed. It is very helpful, again, to have all boxes which you have packed, labeled with where they need to be placed in your new home.

MOVING COMPANIES

William C. Huff Moving and Storage (One of my favorites)
26 Colonial Way, Barrington, NH 03825 800.247.5564
email: Matt@wchuffmoving.com
http://www.wchuffmoving.com

Climate Controlled Storage. Climate controlled storage is a must when storing your items long and short term. Items that are not stored at a climate-controlled facility are at risk of acquiring damage from mold, insects and rapid temperature changes. At William C. Huff Moving and Storage they offer two state of the art storage facilities, one located in Naples, Florida and one in Barrington, New Hampshire. Both of their facilities are clean, neat and alarmed 24 hours a day, 7 days a week.

Packing and Crating. William C. Huff Moving and Storage has experienced staff that can pack the most delicate breakables. Whether it's just a few lamps and pictures or an entire household, they can make the stressful task of "packing" a lot easier. They also offer in-house custom crate building for expensive art, heavy glass, marble and large painting.

Moving Supplies. Often their customers like to pack some possessions or their entire household. Instead of trying to collect boxes at the local grocers or going to over-priced retail stores, their clients can get all of their packing supplies from them. Boxes, tape, clean paper, bubblewrap, tape guns, etc. can be delivered or picked up right at their offices. When purchasing boxes through them you are only charged for what you use. In other words if you buy 20 boxes and only use 10, they will take the unused boxes back and you will not be charged.

A Perfect Move
240 US Route One, Kittery, ME 03804
Phone: 866-630-6740
Website: www.aperfectmove.com

Jobs based on hourly rate – depends on number of movers & number of trucks required for the job. The only charges that you will incur will be the packing (if required) and the move. All services leading up to your move are free of charge.

Wood Brothers Moving and Storage
3607 Lafayette Road, Portsmouth, NH 03801
Phone: 603-436-2725
Website: www.woodbrosmoving.com

Liberty Bell Moving and Storage
249 Islington St #3, Portsmouth, NH 03801
Phone: 603-680-1018
Website: http://libertybellmoving.com/nh

McLaughlin Transportation Systems
75 Constitution Ave, Portsmouth, NH03801
Phone: 603-436-1605
Website: http://www.mcmoving.com/portsmouth-nh.php
Email: Info@mcmoving.com

United Mayflower Storage & Moving
75 Constitution Ave, Portsmouth, NH 03801
Phone: 603-707-4074
Website: http://www.united mayflower.com

A to Z Express Moving & Storage
Portsmouth, NH 03801
Phone: 603-433-6560
Website: http://www.atozexpress.com/

Chapter 8
Assisting Aging Parents

There comes a time as our parents age that they may need to change their current living situation because of changes in their health or their finances. As you visit, be aware of changes that you see in your parents and how they are living in their home. **Here is a list of some of the changes to be aware of:**

1. Is their property maintained the way it always has been?
2. Are there unopened bills and other pieces of mail?
3. Is their ability to get around declining? Has their personal hygiene changed?
4. Do they have vision or hearing loss?
5. Do they have memory loss, frequently repeated stories, or confusion?
6. Are they preoccupied with finances or having unusual spending habits like buying items on infomercials?
7. Are they living more isolated than usual?
8. Do they need assistance with medicines and daily living activities like bathing or cooking?

It is never too early to start to plan for the inevitable. One of the first steps in helping your folks is to begin a diary or notebook of behaviors or concerns. Also begin conversations with your siblings on how you all can assist your parents going forward. Most people wait until a crisis happens and the process at that time is so much harder with all the emotion and urgency attached.

Begin with a plan to help Mom and Dad organize the paperwork and have all necessary legal forms up to date.

I don't think most parents want to leave their children an overwhelming task of settling their estate after they are gone; however, it is hard for most people to want to deal with the reality of their own death. I had always thought that my parents would resist my efforts to help them get all their paperwork and finances in order. I thought their pride and sense of privacy would have them reject my offer to help them. I found instead that when I gave them a list of all the items we needed to have in an organized booklet, they were very relieved. I made a copy of this booklet for my parents and a copy for at least one of their children.

I suggest that one member of the family begin the process by helping Mom and Dad organize the paperwork. Begin by making a list of all the items you want them to gather together. Mail or deliver this list to your parents and ask them to locate and put in one box all of the following items.

Things to organize

Legal Documents: current documents, if they exist and where they are if held elsewhere
1. Will
2. Revocable living Trust
3. POA

4. Living Will
5. List of special bequests

Health Care
1. Durable POA for Health Care
2. Contact info for Physicians/Hospitals
3. Contact info for Dentist
4. Medicaid numbers
5. Medicare
6. Is there a Do Not Recussitate Order and do family members and doctors know of their wishes?

Insurance
All Insurance Policies - Copy of it, Location, Contact info, Account numbers
1. Life
2. Property
3. Auto
4. Long Term Care
5. Other Special Death Benefits
6. Supplementary Health Insurance info
7. Flood insurance?

Income information
1. Pension info/ details
2. SS numbers and income
3. Investment income

Assets and Accounts
1. Combination to the safe, location of any safe deposit boxes
2. List of check and saving accounts, CDs, Money markets
3. List of Credit Cards
4. Brokerage Account Records (stocks and bonds)
5. Annuities, Stock options, Profit sharing
6. Location of recent income tax returns

7. Deeds to all real estate owned. Do they have a title insurance policy? If it is a Condo get copies of rules and regulations, and copies of any mortgages against these properties.
8. Titles to cars
9. List of stored or loaned valuable possessions
10. All Bills regularly paid, dates due and account numbers.
11. Birth Certificates
12. Military discharge papers, Passports
13. Keys to everything they own... safe deposit box, cars, houses, investment properties

Support
1. List of friends to contact to help
2. Organizations that provide services
3. Contact info for Lawyer, Financial Planner, Accountant

End of life
1. List of friends to contact with information on funeral, etc.
2. Funeral/Burial Wishes
3. Are there any personal items that you want specific children to have?
4. Are there any personal items that you want specific siblings to have?
5. Do you want your cars given to any place or person in need?
6. Any special charities you wish money to be donated to?
7. If one of you died and the other needs care, where would each of you like to be moved to?
8. Organ Donor?
9. List of organizations belonged to, other info for Obituary

**BONUS: Go to www.MovingOutMadeEasy.com
to get a copy of this form to use with your parents.**

If you find some important forms like wills, power of attorney for health care or trusts have not yet been created here is an estate planning/elder law specialist in the area I would recommend meeting with:

WILLIAM S BOESCH
Robinson, Boesch, Sennott and Masse, PA
195 New Hampshire Ave
Suite 255
Portsmouth, NH 03801
Phone: 603-427-5380
Email: Wboesch@nhprobatelaw.com

Once they have collected together the vast majority of this information for you, get together with your parents and go to a copy center with at least 2 Large loose leaf binders filled with clear plastic sleeves for each of these numbered items.

Make at least two copies of every insurance policy, bank statement, social security statement, medical card etc on the list and separate them into the categories above. Leave the originals with your parents, plus leave one binder with everything you copied in their home, organized so that it is all in one place. Be sure at least one child or legal representative has a complete set of all this information also.

Be sure to also include a page with all the **contact information on all the beneficiaries** of the will, insurance policies etc. Have their name, address, and phone numbers in one place.

NOTE: While you are putting the booklet together, why don't you do your children a favor and make a booklet for yourself at the same time?

Financial summary

I found that my parents were actually very happy to have me pour through every income statement, pension plan, insurance policy etc and summarize it for them in one place. I listed all the income they had from every source at the present time. I also checked the details of their pension plans to let them know how much income Mom would have if Dad passed away first and how much income Dad would have if Mom passed away first.

Knowing this information is very important as they weigh senior housing options, which can be very expensive.

Meet together with all the siblings

It is critical that siblings all meet together to discuss issues that will come up in the future and let everyone say what is on their minds. This can be an emotional conversation with varied opinions so meeting in a restaurant may help to keep emotions in check. Here are some suggested rules for this introductory meeting:

1. Just invite siblings... leave spouses and grandchildren out of the initial discussion
2. Let everyone go around the table and say what is on their mind before anyone is allowed to comment or ask further questions.
3. Each member of the family comes from different financial and life circumstances so a team approach to assisting parents is a great idea. Let each member state how they might be most able to assist Mom and Dad going forward. Here are some sample suggestions:
   • Provide financial support

- Provide assistance with home maintenance and installing safety features like ramps and grab bars in the home
- Visit, prepare meals, do laundry
- Have Mom and/or Dad move in with them or go live with your parents to offer assistance
- Offer help understanding and completing medical claims and bills
- Offer help with legal forms, bill paying etc.
- Transport or attend doctor appointments and/ serve as medical POA
- Assist in process of sorting through and downsizing their possessions
- Organize community resources to help
- Research senior housing options
- Hold the conversation with Mom and Dad
- Take Mom and Dad to a lawyer to create or update all necessary legal documents like wills, trusts, power of Attorney etc.

Begin the conversation with Mom and Dad

When you start to see signs of decline in your parent's health it is often best to have an impartial professional give you some objective input.   Professional geriatric care managers can be contacted to help you understand the process. It is critical that the person having the conversation with Mom and Dad be able to state their concerns and questions clearly and unemotionally. This is not the best assignment for the drama queen in your family. Here are a few guidelines:

1. Treat your parents with respect and love.

2. Ask your parents questions rather than telling them what you think they need to do.

3. Talk to your parents not about the fact that you think they need to move or how their finances are holding up...instead have more open ended conversations about how they would like to live out the rest of their lives. Ask what they still really enjoy and what has become a burden to them and work on a plan from that perspective.

4. One of the comments we made that resonated with my parents was "Most of us live under the incorrect assumption that our lives will continue along just as they are and then one day we will die. We don't take into consideration the probability that we will have gradually diminishing strength, energy, mobility, financial resources or mental capacity. A move is so much harder and much more overwhelming the longer it is put off."

5. Share concerns of specific events you have noted in your diary that cause concern, and ask your parents if they share your concerns, and if so, what they think they would like to do about it. Suggest other solutions and ask for their thoughts on those options.

6. Most parents really value their independence and the decision to give up that independence in the family home to move into an assisted living facility does not come easily. Do not try to convince them that they will be better off there than in their home, but instead point out the benefits that the new housing option offers.

7. If your parents agree that it is time to sell the family homestead and move, have a prepared list of things that are most important to them in a new home and search for options that meet those criteria. These criteria will be things like monthly cost, geographic location, size of unit in terms of BRs and baths, special amenities or programs like a pool,

garden plots, male/female resident ratios, meal plans or medical assistance.

8. Schedule a time frame in which they agree to visit the suitable housing options and put the family homestead on the market.

When the decision has been made to sell the family home

Selling the family home is a very emotional process for the parents as well as the children. There are memories attached to every corner of the home and yard for both parents and children. It is very important that children do not ask parents to hang onto the home for them unless they are prepared to purchase it at this time. It is a hard enough decision without children adding additional guilt to the process.

For most older parents from the Greatest Generation you will find that they never threw anything away. In order to sell the home the "stuff" is going to have to be disposed of prior to the sale if you want to get top dollar. Check out the chapters on selling and donating unwanted items. Here are some additional suggestions as you get ready to put the home on the market:

1. Find a realtor that your parents trust. There is a realtor designation called Senior Real Estate Specialist which denotes agents who have been trained in how to assist seniors with real estate transitions.

2. Because of the emotions tied to the home, it is probably worth paying for an appraisal and a building inspection prior to putting the home on the market, especially if the owners have lived there a long time. This will allow your Mom and Dad to have a more realistic expectation of sales

price and items that a buyer will want to have taken care of prior to closing. It will also give you time to get repairs done prior to closing and will give you a more realistic sense of how much money they will net after closing costs and fix up costs.

3. If the home is dated in terms of decor or has a lot of deferred maintenance, together you will need to determine if you have the funds and the time and energy to fix the home up to net more money or if you need to sell it "as is" to someone who will pay less and fix it up themselves. Selling a home "as is" will make the home out of reach for first time homeowners with limited downpayments, as their available loan programs often do not allow for peeling paint or older wiring etc.

4. Encourage your parents to travel light to their next home. Don't try to take everything they own with them. It rarely fits, you don't use it and you just have to get rid of it later. Ask your parents to separate out the furnishing, clothing, pots and pans, memorabilia, etc that they really want to take with them no matter what and then have family or professionals assist them in getting rid of the remaining items. Those raised during the Great Depression have a terrible time throwing anything away and this becomes the most overwhelming part of the move. Try to find a home for the serviceable items. One of the major reasons to help your parents with selling or donating the possessions which will not go with them in the move is the large number of people who take advantage of the elderly through scams or theft.

Although traveling light is the way to go, the reality is that your parents will probably want to take more than will comfortably fit in their new space. Sometimes they want to take items like golf clubs or gardening tools with them because it is still part of their identity. Don't press too hard about the need to get rid of these items before the move if it is causing a lot of resistance. Sometimes it takes being in the new space for them to realize there is no longer room for these items and that they really are not using them anymore. Whether they completely downsize before the move or do it in a two-step process, further downsizing once they are in the new housing space is not that important in the big picture of their life. Either way it will happen, or they may just prefer to live with their unused golf clubs in the corner of the living room.

5. Don't try to make the current furniture fit in the new downsized space. It was purchased for a different living situation. Budget some money for some new furnishings which fit the new space and have fun creating a new environment for the next phase of the journey.

6. Decide if your parents can handle physically, emotionally and financially staying in the home while it is being marketed or if they can move into their new housing prior to marketing the home. Try to picture the online video of the home if there are walkers and hospital beds in the living room. Determine if they can really keep the home suitable for showings on short notice and pick up and leave for showings at all hours of the day.

7. Once the home is under agreement and items come up during the appraisal or inspection process, help your parents determine the options, but leave the final decisions to them. Being asked to decide what to do about replacement of the old roof or septic system is too complex and overwhelming for older people to evaluate effectively. My parents appreciated us coming up with two well thought-out

options, explaining the costs, and pluses and minuses of each option, but leaving the final decision of which path to pursue to them, so that they still felt in charge.

Assisting your parents in a transition from the family home to a more suitable housing situation for their age and health is a very complicated scenario. Expect that it will take some time for your parents to adjust to the new quarters, as change is hard for anyone, and especially hard the longer we have lived in one place. This chapter just touches on the subject. If you are struggling with this process please reference the other books on these topics at the end of my book.

Chapter 9
Special Tips for the Special Ones in your Life

How to Settle an Estate without unsettling the family

If you are lucky, your parents took the advice given earlier in the book and had a will, organized records and had purged their lifetime of possessions, and the process of settling their estate will be more streamlined.

Unfortunately, approximately half of Americans with children die without a will, and if they didn't take a few hours to make a will, it is unlikely that all their financial and legal records are in order and that they have sorted and disposed of their extra possessions. If there was a valid will, be sure to read it carefully as some people list specific items they would like to have specific people have after they are gone. These wishes should be honored, if at all possible.

An executor of the estate must be named in the will or appointed by the court.

Once your parent's debts have been paid, all heirs have been notified and the net worth of the estate is established, the division of personal property can begin and this is unfortunately where most of the discord in families begins.

I have found that families that handle this process the best all come together and each take responsibility for a part of the process of sorting, cleaning, repairing and disposing of items in the home. Some people contribute manual labor, some sort and organize and clean, some do bookkeeping of expenses and some hire help that is needed. It is especially important if siblings have differing amounts of time and money, to give each person a task that fits their available time and income, and to value the contribution each is able to make. Someone giving up 3 Saturdays to sort through boxes in the basement can be just as important as the sibling who lives further away, but offers to pay for a cleaning service or legal help.

It is not always that important that everyone gets exactly the same number of items from the home, but each should have an equal chance to select items that have value or meaning to them. If there are a few items in the home which have significantly more monetary value like a car, a rare painting, a coin collection or large pieces of furniture, these items are often sold for fair market value and the cash is divided equally before heirs start selecting specific items they would like, unless one of the heirs is willing to purchase that item with cash or their share of the anticipated inheritance.

I have seen entire families come to the house together and have everyone draw a number, including grandchildren old enough to participate. Then starting with whoever has number one, each person selects an item in the home they would like to keep. It may be a piece of jewelry, the handprint mold they made as a child or the dining room set. These items are then put on a list as belonging to that person after the home is sold and emptied out. Each person from say 1 to 15 selects their item in order and then you start onto round two, this time starting with #15 and selecting items in reverse order. This zigzag method of selecting items continues until no one wants any further items. One person may only want 3 items and another may want 12 items before they stop selecting items. In many families with fully furnished homes, no one may be interested in the furniture and it may need to be sold or donated.

I have found that often those siblings with more personal assets are more interested in selecting items that hold special sentimental value and are okay that someone else takes the car because they really need a car, even though it is worth more . It is usually a good idea BEFORE you begin selecting items to determine if the item you selected will be given an approximate value and subtracted from your share of the remaining estate after the home and other assets are sold or if the items people select will be on top of an equally divided amount of the remaining estate. Determining a system of how the assets will be divided, which is done before a single person starts discussing any particular item they are interested in, seems to be a very important part of keeping the emotions from taking over.

I have also found that some families like to select items they think close friends of the deceased would like as a remembrance of their parents.

Moving with Children

- Know that change is hard and focus on the positives of the new move, ie. they get their own bedroom, live near the playground, house has a hot tub or pool, etc.
- Let children have input into decorating their new room in terms of paint colors, maybe a new bedspread or computer.
- Very small children need to have someone assigned to care for them or they need to stay with a friend on moving-in day so that parents can direct the movers.

- At the end of moving in day, take a break, go to the park, get an ice cream, let kids burn off some energy.
- Teens need to stay connected so get computers set up and let them contact their friends to discuss the move.
- If you are driving a long way to your new home, create a bag of inexpensive "dollar store" treats and toys to open every 100 miles. This gives kids something to look forward to during the long drive.
- I moved many times as a child. Without a doubt the hardest day of all is the first day you walk into your new school alone, not knowing a soul. If you have any ability to speak with your child's teachers before the first day of school, I would ask if there is a student in class that they feel would be willing to meet your child at the bus or the door and stay with them the first day. That would mean introducing them to others at recess, making sure they know how to get to every classroom and inviting them to sit with them at lunchtime. The next day they are on their own, but at least they have met a few people on day one and don't feel so alone.
- Many parents believe it is easier for their children to move at the end of the school year. I do not believe this always to be true. If you move at the end of the school year, your children will have at least two months in a new place where they may not know anyone and will have few opportunities to meet others. It can be a very, very long lonely summer. Also they will now be starting the new school on the first day of school when everyone is connecting with their friends they haven't seen all summer and newcomers get very little attention. If you move mid-year, your children will be the new kids on the block and they will be noticed. School activities will be going on and there will be many activities for them to meet other kids with similar interests. If your child has an interest that is very important to them like being on the football team or in the school play, I would check with

the new school and find out what time frames are necessary for them to be able to participate in those important activities and aim for those dates, even if you need to go to the new home a bit early or let them finish out the sports season while living with a friend.

- Do not dismiss the importance of a friend that your child is leaving. My sister moved from Boston to Chicago at the end of kindergarten. My parents made arrangements for her to visit this friend nearly every year. Back in those days there were no cell phones, no skype, no email.... just handwritten letters to stay in touch. They never lived anywhere close to each other for the rest of their lives, but she was the maid of honor in my sister's wedding 25 year later. I'm sure you can set up facetime or skype, or visits with important friends. Most friendships will fade away with time, but some will stand the test of time.

Moving with Pets

- Plan for the pets weeks in advance. Most dogs and cats will go through moving anxiety, so be sure to plan time for walks and play time during the packing and moving process.
- Watch for any changes in their behavior and eating and sleeping habits. Schedule a pre-move appointment with your vet. Be sure all vaccinations are current and carry proof of shots. Airlines will require health certificates from a licensed vet within 10 days of transporting them by air. Dogs and cats will need to be at least 8 weeks old and weaned to travel by air. Airlines can refuse to transport any animal for any reason so be sure to check with them on complete kennel requirements, etc.
- If you will be driving with pets in the car, start with short drives and increase the time to longer drives. If they do not do well they may need to be sedated for the trip and you will need to order drugs from the vet now.

- Travel supplies should include water, food, bowls, can opener if needed, leash, bedding, poop bags or litter box.
- Feed your pet three hours before the trip and take them for a walk right before leaving. At stops provide water, a walk and maybe a treat. Never leave pets in a parked car on a warm day. You may need to plan to pack picnic meals so that you can feed yourself without leaving the pets in the car. Feed your pet upon arrival at your destination each day.
- Search for pet friendly accommodations at www.pets welcome.com.
- It is best to kennel your pets or find a neighbor to care for them on both moving-out and moving-in day. There will be so many people coming and going, and doors opening, that there is a high probability of a pet slipping away. The chaos is also often upsetting to pets used to a certain routine.
- Birds, gerbils, hamsters and reptiles generally travel well in their cages in the car. To avoid drafts it is best to cover the cage during travel. Be sure to give water at every stop as it may spill during the drive and they can get dehydrated very easily.

Chapter 10
Who Needs to Know about my Move?

The following people need to be notified regarding the utilities for the house:

Electricity company
Telephone company
Oil or Gas Company
Water Company
Sewer Company
Pest/ Termite Company
Cable company (return cable box and remotes if part of service)
Internet (return modem if part of service)
Garbage
Security system

Government Agencies
Change of address at the Post office
Cancel current PO Box and order to start at new address 2 weeks early
IRS
Social Security Administration
Motor Vehicle Registrations
Driver's License
Professional Licenses

Financial groups
Accountant
Bank Accounts
1. Change all automatic deposits and withdrawals 30 days ahead if you are closing accounts.
2. Don't forget to transport items in safe deposit box to new bank.
3. If not changing banks you still need to order new checks with new address and have statements mailed to new address or new email.

Credit Cards
1. Cancel cards to local stores.
2. Notify other accounts of change of address.
3. If you are not sure which cards you still have open, ask to see a copy of your credit report and it will list all open accounts which need to be notified or closed.

Loan Accounts
1. If your current home has a mortgage that is not being assumed it will be paid off (hopefully with the proceeds of the sale of your home).
2. If you have mortgages on other properties which are not the home you are selling, they need to be notified of change of address.
3. If you have an Equity Credit line on the home you are selling with no outstanding balance, return checks and close account out prior to closing or they may withhold proceeds at time of closing to pay any checks that might come in.

Investment accounts/ stock broker/ financial planner

Airline mileage Accounts

Workplace personnel etc.

Subscriptions to be changed
Magazines
Newspapers
Newsletters
Book/ CD/ wine/ fruit etc of the month clubs
Catalogs

Medical/Educational Records
Doctors
Hospitals
Dentists
Orthodontists
Pharmacies: Fill all important prescriptions before moving
Health insurance: Get list of approved doctors, etc in new area
Schools: Check procedure for getting school records transferred.
Be sure to register child for new school as soon as possible. Find
out what new school will need in terms of shots, identification
etc.

Other professionals and businesses to be notified
Lawyer
Veterinarian
Auto/ Car/ Home insurance: Do not cancel homeowners on
current dwelling until you have arrived and inspected goods at
new home
House cleaners
Lawn maintenance
Snow plow providers
Dry cleaners: Make sure you have picked everything up
Public Library: Return all books and DVDs before they get
packed or tossed out
Church
Health club/ sport club: All memberships cancelled, uniforms
returned

Personally connected Individuals
Family
Friends
Colleagues
Babysitter/ Daycare
Hairdresser

Sample forms to notify groups of move

Utility

This notice is to inform you that as of (date) _____

will no longer be at (address) _____

My account number is _____

I would like to order a final meter reading or fill for (date) ___
and have the final bill sent to me at my new address _____.

The new owner or occupant of this property will be _____.

If they have not changed the service into their names as of
(date) _____ please cancel the service.

Signed _____

Name_____

Phone or email_____

Moving Out Made Easy

Sample notification for Government and Financial services

This notice is to inform you that as of (date) _____

will no longer be at (address) _____

My account number is _____

1. ___ As of that date please transfer all correspondence to my new address at _____.

2. ___ I will be coming in on (date) _____ to close my accounts and would appreciate all necessary forms ready.

3. ___ Please send me all necessary paperwork to transfer my accounts to (mail or email address) _____.

Signed _____

Name_____

Phone or email_____

Sample notification for Subscriptions/ Catalogs/ Etc.

This notice is to inform you that as of (date) _____

will no longer be at (address/email) _____

___ I would like my service changed to my new address at
_____.

___ I would like to cancel my service at this time and have any prepaid fees refunded to my new address at _____.

Signed _____

Name_____

Phone or email_____

Change of address:
https://moversguide.usps.com/icoa/move-info   or   use   the
following to mail to the following people

Dear

I just wanted to let you know that as of _____ I/we
will no longer be at _____.

As   of   _____   we   can   be   reached   in   the
following ways:

Mailing Address

_____

_____

Email Address _____

Home Phone _____

Mobile Phone _____

Social Media:

Facebook _____

Linked in _____

Twitter _____

Website _____

Other _____

Chapter 11
How to Make your New House Feel like Home

Projects that are easiest to do before you move in

If you have the ability to stay in your current home for a few days before moving into your new home, these projects are so much easier and sometimes less expensive to have done while the home is empty.

1. Flooring- Try to refinish any hardwood floor, install new carpet or new flooring.
2. Sanding and painting- Plaster dust goes everywhere and walls and ceilings are much easier to patch and paint when the room is empty.
3. Organization systems for the closets, basement, garage- Now is the time to add extra rods in the closet before the clothes need to be hung up. Install shelving units in the basement, set up a workbench for your tools and install hooks or racks for sporting and garden equipment.

Securing your new home

1. Be sure to change locks or rekey all locks to the home (you have no idea who still has a key to your new home).
2. Be sure all family members have keys to the new home.

3. Be sure you have smoke detectors and carbon monoxide detectors on all levels of your home.
4. Don't forget to make a plan to take care of the items the building inspector found in your home that needed attention.
5. Install or sign up for an alarm security system. (Be sure to notify insurance company as it should reduce your premium.)

Unpacking and Disposal of Packing Materials

1. If at all possible plan to stay at a hotel the first night so that there is not the extra stress of setting up beds and cooking dinner etc after a long tiring day.
2. Unpack your "open me first" survival boxes then follow the suggested order below.
3. Hook up telephone and plug in cell phones in their chargers.
4. Locate lamps and plug them in so that you have lights in every room before it gets dark.
5. Hook up televisions, computers and appliances like refrigerator and washer and dryer.
6. Put beds together and make up beds and put linens away.
7. Put food and kitchen supplies away.
8. Empty wardrobe boxes and empty clothing boxes.
9. Put away video games, videos, DVDs, tapes and CDs.
10. Put away books and toys and all sports equipment.
11. Put away good china, knickknacks, hang pictures, mirrors etc.
12. Organize seasonal decorations, tools, garage and basement items and outdoor furniture.

Professional moving boxes cost a lot of money but also take up a lot of space to store. To store for a future move, to sell or give away on Craig's list or to recycle to a friend or recycling center these boxes must be broken down and stacked neatly.

1. Break boxes down as you unpack them.
2. Store them in one location in large unbroken-down box to keep them from sliding around.
3. They must be kept dry so do not put them in a damp basement or on a garage floor where rain and snow from cars will ruin their value.
4. Be sure to look carefully at all paper left in boxes to be sure no small items are left among the packing materials.
5. Smooth packing papers out and stack in unbroken-down boxes.
6. Movers can be asked to remove all packing materials and boxes from the property if it is part of your contract. If not ask your realtor if they know someone who would like them.

Become a Resident

1. Register to vote.
2. Get a new driver license and license plates if you have changed states.
3. Shop for the best cable, internet and phone service providers.
4. Find a lawyer and revise your will, trust etc to reflect your new property.
5. Get new bank checks with your new address.
6. Get a license for your dog if your community licenses dogs or other pets.

Make new friends, but keep the old.

Having moved frequently during my lifetime, I have found that the new house never really feels like home until you have found some friends in your new neighborhood. We all have very different personalities and comfort levels in this skill of making friends, but the following are some of the best ways that I have found to meet the people most likely to have things in common with you to form the basis of a new friendship.

Pets: Nothing seems to get strangers to stop and talk with you like walking a dog. It is something that you can do every day, morning noon and night. It gets you out of the house, gets fresh air in your lungs and is great exercise for both you and your four legged best friend. You will find that people tend to have regular routes and times to walk so you should quickly start to recognize the neighbors and their dogs. If there is a local dog park, go there and chat with other dog owners while the dogs play. You can always talk about your dogs, no matter how shy you are about making conversation.

Young Children: Just like walking dogs, pushing babies and toddlers in a stroller is a good way to find other parents with similar aged children. Go to the local playgrounds and talk with other moms and dads about what activities their children enjoy in the community and take your children to those playgroups, story hours at the library, gymboree classes, etc. Ask if there are any babysitting coops or babysitters they recommend. As you start to meet the same parents on a regular basis, ask if they might want to come over for pizza and let the kids play together on a Friday night.

School Age Children: Once your children are in school, try to find time to volunteer in the classroom or attend PTA meetings and volunteer for projects they are sponsoring. Try to attend as many of your children's sporting activities and chat with other parents in the stands. If your schedule makes you more available to drive than other parents, offer to drive neighborhood children on your child's team home after a practice or game. Ask your children which kids they have met that they would like to get to know better and call the parents and introduce yourself and ask if the kids can get together to play at your home. You may be interested in helping with Scouting activities or other after school enrichment programs like FFA or Destination Imagination.

Realize that your kids may miss their old friends and allow opportunities for them to get together with old friends, or go back to visit or just connect online.

Community Involvement: Every town has opportunities to get involved in activities you enjoy. Many communities have Newcomer Clubs filled with other people looking for new friends. Search the website of your local community or go into town hall and ask about all the committees and organizations that are available to join. It may be the local garden club, the bridge group, the beach walkers, trustees of the library, the local Republican or Democrat etc committee, coaching or helping with the fields for the youth recreation department. There may be book of the month clubs, opportunities to volunteer at performances at local theaters or concerts, or groups that help the elderly with rides to doctor's appointments or visit nursing homes with their pets, or groups that help the homeless. Lonely as you might feel if you have moved to a totally new location, there are always people who would love to have you share your special talents, be it reading, music, theatre, sports, cooking, etc. Remember that focusing your conversation on how unhappy you are or how your former community was better will drive people away, not attract new friends to you. If you expect to find friendly people in your new town, I guarantee you will find them.

When I did a home exchange in the Cotswolds of England for 4 weeks, I actually went door to door and said I was hosting a meet the neighbors dinner on Friday night and hoped they would attend. I made a large salad and two crock pots of soup and a batch of cookies and ended up with a simple dinner party with 10 people in attendance. After that one party, I was invited to local cocktail parties, over for lunch, to join ladies craft night and to join the local women's group on their monthly outing for dinner and Skittles which was a simple bowling game. At the end of 4 weeks I was told I knew more people in the village than some of the local residents, simply because I took a chance and knocked on a few doors and invited the neighbors over.

Special Interests: When you first move to an area it is a great time to take a class or join a group to explore an interest you have had, but never had time to get involved with. Now would be a great time to take a watercolor painting class once a week, or join a gym with regular exercise classes or sign up for a cooking class. If there is anything you have an interest in, just look for a meetup group online that is interested in the activity you enjoy. There are meetup groups for kayakers, hikers, singles, knitters, poets, dining out groups etc; simply sign up and you will get emails of all the activities they are joining in to enjoy together. If you are an empty-nester when you move, look for programs and field trips sponsored by the Community or Senior Center, for educational series at local colleges or for do it yourself classes at places like Home Depot. Most of these groups are full of people who do not know each other, and you can always find someone new to strike up a conversation with as you enjoy the hike or join in an activity.

Churches, Synagogues, Etc.: I have found that finding a church home is a wonderful weekly place to meet others with similar interests. Small churches are usually more apt to notice new people and approach them. Large churches are more apt to have organized small groups like small group suppers, classes or bible studies to help people to connect and share their faith together. If the first house of faith you visit doesn't feel like home, keep looking. There are so many types of worship today that if you look long enough and also ask others for recommendations you should be able to find a church community that feels like home.

Make a plan to stay in touch with good friends or family members in your former location. It is important to make plans to visit or skype or facetime with those who have been important to you or your children. Plans may include returning to your former town for a visit or scheduling a vacation or activity midway between the towns where you can spend time together with your friends to have some fun together. Having a future visit to look forward to makes it easier to say goodbye, knowing it is not forever.

Other books to read for more information on various topics touched upon in this book

Overall Moving Tips

Organize, Pack, Move by Nancy Giehl and Joan Hobbs.... Strategies and Money Saving Ideas to Simplify your move.

The Moving Survival Guide by Martha Poage ... All you need to know to make your move go smoothly

How to Survive a Move by Hundreds of Heads... Stories and tips of those who have moved

29 Days to a Smooth Move by Donna Kozik and Tara Maras ...Save your Cents, Save your Sanity and Save Scads of Your time

Slick Move Guide by Jodi J Velazquez...Secrets You Need to Know if You are Moving

Sell, Keep or Toss? by Harry L. Rinker.... How to Downsize a Home, Settle an Estate or Appraise Personal Property.

Downsizing and Senior Moves

Downsizing Made Easy by Nikki Bucklew 5 Easy Steps to a successful move

The Boomer Burden by Julie Hall, the Estate Lady.... Dealing with your Parent's Lifetime Accumulation of Stuff

Don't Toss My Memories in the Trash, A Step-by-Step to Helping Seniors Downsize, Organize and Move by Vickie Dellaquila, a professional organizer and senior move manager.

The Moving Workbook by Vickie Dellaquila is also available

No Ordinary Move by Barbara Z Perrman, Ph.D and Jim Ballard ... Relocating your Aging Parents, A Guide for Boomers

Moving in the Right Direction by Bruce Nemovitz..... The Senior's Guide to Moving and Downsizing

Moving for Seniors by Barbara H Morris....... Household downsizing and estate dispersal

The Upside of Downsizing by Karen O'Connor ...... 50 Ways to create a cozy life

How to Clean Out Your Parent's Estate in 30 days or Less by Julie Hall, the Estate Lady ... A solutions-based guide to emptying the home without losing your mind.

Moving with Children

Moving with Kids by Lori Collins Burgan.... 25 Ways to Ease your Family's Transition to a New Home

About Nancy Beveridge

Nancy Beveridge, a long time resident of North Hampton, NH is the mother of two lovely daughters who were raised in the Seacoast area of New Hampshire. She is also a proud grandmother with a young granddaughter and grandson.

Nancy is the team leader of the Seacoast Sold Team, the leading residential sales team at Coldwell Banker Residential Brokerage in Portsmouth, NH. Nancy has been in real estate sales for 34 years and has a team with an additional 25 years of real estate experience. She also owns 11 rental properties as an investor and won the 2012 Entrepreneur of the Year Award. She serves on the Professional Standards Board of the Seacoast Board of Realtors, is the Events and Education director of the North Hampton Business Association, the founder of the Seacoast Social Club and a graduate of Tony Robbin's Mastery University, Rich Dad Education, the Wealth Forum and Brian Buffini's Peak Producers. Her website is www.SeacoastSold .com. Client testimonials can be found at www.SeacoastSold TeamReviews.com and recommended contractors and professionals can be found at www.OnlineReferral Directory.com.

Awards
- Named One of Top Realtors for exceptional service by NH Magazine
- N E Previews Incredible Service Award for Luxury Home Sales- 2004
- International President's Elite Award, Coldwell Banker
- Realtor Online Marketing Award of Excellence
- Peak Producer Ambassador
- Over $225 million in sales

Education & Certification
- e-Pro Certification
- Seniors Real Estate Specialist, NAR
- Certified Buyer Representative
- Certified Home Marketing Specialist
- New Homes Specialist
- Certified Internet Marketing Specialist
- Certified Distressed Property Expert
- Certified Negotiation Specialist
- Certified Residential Relocation Specialist
- Notary Public

Contact Information
Email: Team@SeacoastSold.com
Phone: 603-765-2663
Website: www.SeacoastSold.com
Client comments: www.SeacoastSoldTeamReviews.com

45812700R00075

Made in the USA
Middletown, DE
14 July 2017